Occupation:

NEST BUILDER

JUDY HAMMERSMARK

ACCENT BOOKS
Denver, Colorado

MEMBER OF
EVANGELICAL CHRISTIAN
PUBLISHERS ASSOCIATION

Some of the material in this book appeared in partial or similar form as articles in the following publications, which held first magazine rights:

Portions of Chapter One appeared under the title, "Occupation: Nestbuilder" in *Life and Health,* May, 1979.

Portions of Chapter Two appeared under the title, "A Mother's Dilemma" in *Today's Christian Mother,* Spring, 1977.

Chapter Three appeared as "God Bless Me" in a 1979 issue of *These Times.*

Chapter Seven appeared as "Our Crusade Against Clutter" in Life and Health, August, 1978.

Chapter Eight appeared as "Importance of Prayer" in *Today's Christian Mother,* Fall, 1976.

Chapter Nine appeared as "Dignity In Small Packages" in *Baby Talk,* April, 1978.

Chapter Eleven appeared as "Helping Your Child Deal With Angry Feelings" in *Christian Herald,* January, 1979.

Chapter Twelve appeared as "Now She Is Ready" in *Today's Christian Mother,* Summer, 1975.

Chapter Fifteen appeared as "Wanting Is Worth Waiting" in *Today's Christian Mother,* Winter, 1972.

ACCENT BOOKS
A division of Accent-B/P Publications, Inc.
12100 W. Sixth Avenue
P.O. Box 15337
Denver, Colorado 80215

Library of Congress Catalog Card Number: 78-74203

ISBN O-89636-020-2

Contents

*This book is lovingly dedicated
to "Chief Eagle" Marvin
and
three precious fledglings,
John, Jacque, and Kirsten*

What This Book Is About

It is July, 1963. The early morning sun filters through the curtains as I hurriedly finish feeding my two month old son. I burp, bathe and dress his squirming little frame. He turns a funny little face to me, cooing sweetly. *No time for conversation now.* I must get to work!

I rush to the kitchen, pop two slices of bread into the toaster and start the morning coffee. By 7:30, breakfast is over and my husband is off to his job.

As I struggle to squeeze myself, diaper bag, baby-in-infant-seat into the front seat of the car, I wonder, *is it all worth it?*

8:00 a.m.: My son is safely with his sitter, and I am at my office typing. My mind wanders. I wonder how my little one is getting along with the sitter. Will he get his first tooth today? All morning it plays on my mind that I missed his first smile and today I may also miss his first tooth!

By noon I am convinced that all this is sheer madness. I call my husband to tell him I am quitting my job. As usual, he is understanding.

"We'll manage somehow," he tells me.

OCCUPATION: NESTBUILDER

How universal is my dilemma? How many women go through what I have gone through, wondering which my family needs more, my presence or another paycheck?

For a long time I have been thinking that our society does not fully appreciate the contribution of women at home. In reality, the keeper of the domestic flame is a vital, powerful person. She wears many hats in her complex undertaking as wife and mother. Her job calls for enormous versatility, a wealth of energy, and wisdom—even genius. In one day, a woman of my calling might act as chauffeur, beautician, gardener, consulting psychologist—even undertaker if the family pet should meet with calamity.

In our hands rests the future of our civilization. In our trust the very lives of infants and children are placed. Within our realm of responsibility falls the task of maintaining family health through nutritional consciousness and intelligent meal planning. While husbands look to us for companionship and comfort, our children seek in our presence the wisdom required to deal with an increasingly complex world.

Our services are offered without recompense, for there is no way to place a monetary value on all that women do and are. Our contributions are an offering of love and, therefore, without price. Yet, many are telling us that we are not doing enough. That we must be out in the business world as well, earning and competing.

Who is right? Do women belong in the home or on

the job? Where is womanpower most desperately needed in today's world? Does society no longer require the services of dutiful mothers and wives, women who give their all to home and family?

It is not my aim to belittle anyone or any group of women. We all have much soul-searching and praying to do regarding this dilemma. I am not denigrating women who must work for reasons financial. And my heart goes out to mothers who are alone for one reason or another and find it necessary to provide both a home and a living. Certainly they deserve all our support, love and prayers. And there are other women, wives and mothers, with special skills and training who make a vital contribution to our society; we are all the richer for it. And still other women simply must have the emotional release and the identity that an outside job provides. The purpose of this book is not to minimize the contributions of these women to society.

Rather, my purpose in writing this book is to celebrate the traditional roles of wife and mother, and thus, to elevate them beyond what some believe them to be.

1
HELP WANTED:
Keeper Of The Nest

HELP WANTED: Full-time person; must be good cook, nurse, like kids and animals, be adept at home cleaning and maintenance; have knowledge of basic child and adult psychology; be good with figures, able to balance a checkbook; have skills in gardening and home crafts, furniture refinishing, interior decorating, wallpapering and painting. Those unwilling to put in long hours overtime with little monetary reward need not apply.

So might read a help-wanted ad for my replacement. My job is Homemaker. I look after a three-story house, parent three children between the ages of seven and fifteen, oversee a dog, an occasional tomcat, two hamsters and a thirsty sword fern. I have been happily married to the same man for almost sixteen years.

Although I like my job as wife, mother, and keeper of the house, I have been in the habit of thinking of it as part-time, temporary employment.

OCCUPATION: NESTBUILDER

For years I have been planning to get a paying job uptown whenever all the kids were in school; for some time I have anticipated going back to work.

When I recently announced my plans to my family, my second grader, a bubbly gidget with mischievous, blue-gray eyes and a constellation of freckles across her nose, wanted to know, "But Mommie, who will take your place?"

Her question started my mental wheels turning: *Who could qualify as my replacement?* I took a wary glance backward into my own childhood. As the daughter of a career mother, I recalled the aching emptiness I had felt upon returning from school to a vacant house. *Do I really want that for my children?* I asked myself.

Some recent studies seem to indicate that certain well-organized mothers of nursery-school children actually spend more time with their youngsters than their stay-at-home counterparts. In other words, some stay-at-home mommies are not really doing all that much mothering. Thus, it is easy to rationalize that *quality* of time is what really matters—what you do with your children when you are with them is what really counts.

On the other hand, a child's need for loving support rarely keeps a schedule. Sickness, important events in children's lives, and emotional upsets do not always occur when working mothers are available to proffer praise, sympathy or advice.

Ideally, the combination is quality *and* quantity, offering generous portions of both to the children in our care.

Our society does not emphasize enough the importance of a secure home life in children's lives. According to Dr. James Dobson, Associate Clinical Professor of Pediatrics at the USC School of Medicine and best-selling author, the job of mother/homemaker is of the utmost importance to the health and vitality of our nation as a whole.

"I have developed a deep appreciation for the unique skills required of wives and mothers. I regret the lack of respect and status given today's housewives," he said in a recent interview with a UPI reporter.

As I look at myself and the many women I am acquainted with, it becomes evident that many of us work too hard. Why do we do this? Nobody insists that we be all things to all people. Why can't we relax?

Many of us, I feel, have been unduly influenced by the persuasive propaganda of our day. Much of the rhetoric we hear today over television and radio, and what we read in newspapers and magazines challenges us to find fulfillment outside the home. Keeping family together, we are told, cannot be as creative or as important as work outside. We see, for example, magazine ads and television commercials depicting:

—lovely women entertaining in perfectly decorated homes
—spotless, glimmering linoleum and mothers who never lose their Job-like patience when Junior tracks mud over it

—ladies whose leisure-hour talents include painting, gardening and sewing for one's family
—mothers who communicate with their children while romping across sandy beaches
—wives who are never too busy or too tired to give their undivided time and attention to hubby
—women involved in car pools, women's clubs, charity events, Little League, Girl Scouts
—talented cooks who effortlessly whip up perfect desserts on a moment's notice for their husband's boss
—career women who take business trips, somehow leaving lint-free homes and well-adjusted, self-reliant husbands and children in their wake

The ads look good. We want to be all these things. *We* put pressure on *ourselves* to be all things to all people. Thus, we have been swayed into making unwise choices concerning family and home.

For a long time I *actually* believed with all my heart that in order to qualify as a full-fledged member of the human race, in addition to my home responsibilities, I had to hold down an outside job and be materially compensated for my work. Many of the women I talk with feel this way, too.

It truly takes a strong-minded person to rise above today's school of thought which calls for sabbatical leave for pregnancy, that defines pregnancy as a temporary disability, thus limiting motherhood to the delivery table. No wonder so many are taking their baby leave only to return immediately to the sorority of working mothers!

Just how coincidental this increasingly popular idea is with the decline in society's esteem for the woman at home, I don't know. But just how far we have come in depreciating the woman's most basic part in society was brought home to me when a woman in my husband's office took time off to have her first baby.

Within a few weeks she was back at her desk, telling her co-workers, "I've had my fill of playing dolls."

Another mother left her child with me for a few hours the other afternoon. Much of the afternoon I held him on my lap because every few minutes he would break into quiet sobs.

"Was he good?" the little boy's mother asked upon her return. I told her that he had been good although he did cry occasionally.

"He cries at the day care center, too," she told me. "I'm sorry he was bad."

Our system of values is out of kilter when women rate their jobs over their responsibility to their children.

I have worked sporadically during my child-rearing years, and although I really do miss the extra money my job provided, I believe the things I can offer my children by being home are more important than my extra paycheck. The greatest advantage of the full-time homemaker, I feel, is *time*.

Now that I am not working outside the home, I am usually here when my kids trail in after school.

As I prepare their after-school snack, we have time to talk. Communication of this kind seems to help them sort out their problems. Perhaps this is the most important aspect of a mother's job—being there to listen and to counsel, helping her youngsters maintain high self-esteem by talking out problems as they occur. No matter how impatient I have been at times, I am certain my overall influence has been far superior to the care of the impersonal sitters I paid for while I was working.

Now that I am home, a labor of love is the type of food I prepare. I have time to prepare soups that simmer all afternoon, homemade biscuits, muffins and breads instead of the "quickie" frozen meals, expensive convenience foods, dinners out of a can or package, or—even more expensive—the easy-to-prepare steaks which I made frequent use of when I was working. Now that my agenda is less crowded, I usually prepare a hot breakfast, sending my loved ones away nutritionally fortified for the day.

My husband and I found that the extra expenses associated with my working drastically cut into our financial profits, but the most scrimped-on item during my career days was our intimate relationship. It seemed that as we both became over-involved in meaningful work outside the home, time together was pushed to the bottom of our list of priorities.

Could this loss of involvement with one another account, at least in part, for America's ever-increasing divorce rate? Could it be that too many women working full-time spell disaster for the man/woman relationship? At least one authority,

Dwight Harvey Small, author of *Design For Christian Marriage,* considers this a possibility.

The separation from home of the working mother seems to change women's sense of values. Away from the stabilizing home influence, many venture off into an extended ego trip, only to plunk back to earth too late. For husbands rebel, too, against the strangers their wives become. Broken homes are frequently a side trip of the excursion out of the nest. A successful marital partnership takes an emotional investment for which many overly-busy, preoccupied men and women no longer have the energy.

While working, I began to appreciate another blessing that my formerly relaxed schedule had allowed. Although it takes only a few minutes to brighten the day of a shut-in, I did not make time for that once I began working. There was little time to deepen long-standing friendships. I missed neighborly chats over the backyard fence, front porch talk sessions while the kids ran and played on the grass. Being a good friend and neighbor, I discovered, takes time—something in direly short supply when one works.

I also missed going into my room alone, sometimes in the middle of the afternoon, to talk with God. Before I worked, I had time to pray about a lot of things that troubled me. While working, my prayer life disintegrated; it was reduced to hurried, rambling generalities. No longer did I pray about my mother's heart problem, my sister's family crisis, my country, or our president as he met with world leaders in the hope of securing peace.

OCCUPATION: NESTBUILDER

Truly, the advantages of not working can be reduced to one word—*time*. Yet, the concept of time, all it entails, encompasses every aspect of our daily lives.

It's sad that so many conscientious homemakers have been lumped together in society's view with the truly unproductive housewife. She is often caricatured as lazy, an addict of soap operas and game shows. Seldom does she miss her afternoon nap. She is a real parasite, rarely cooking a good meal for her family, never ironing a shirt or picking up needle and thread to mend.

Certainly, there are many women who are like this, yet there are thousands upon thousands of American women who give their all to make home a pleasant place to return to each evening. I think few people truly appreciate the care and concern of the dedicated, creative homemaker. She provides not just the physical necessities for comfortable living; she offers something intangible, a force in the lives of her family which can only be defined as *spiritual*. The woman at home supplies characteristics by their nature difficult to define, yet essential for the quality and tone of a happy civilization.

For these reasons, I am seriously considering making my temporary, part-time job a permanent one. As I see it, our world has a crying need for women at home. Not housewives, but *homemakers*, women with a calling, persons who strive to maintain an ambiance of peace, love and safety for those in their care.

It has taken me time, but I have come to realize

just how important my profession really is. Not everyone can qualify as keeper of the marital flame, overseer of the kids, builder of the nest!

Yet . . . occasionally the grass still seems greener on the business side of the fence . . .

2
THE NEST:
Here And Now

Our society used to insist that home was the place for women, especially mothers of young children, women like myself who have no immediate calling other than keeper of the flame. But in its headlong pursuit of things material, our modern world has devalued the unique contributions which women make to the home and family, and we are all the poorer for it. It is truly surprising how at times even husbands do not understand and appreciate the value of the woman at home.

Millie Franklin, a pretty, blue-eyed mother of four, was on the verge of tears. "Harold thinks I should go to work!" she told me. Millie and Harold had recently finished building their new home, and Harold was urging Millie to get a job "to help pay off the mortgage in ten years instead of twenty."

"I realize how much another paycheck would help, but I just can't stand the idea of leaving my new home all day after all that we've put into it," she told me.

Millie finally convinced her hubby that her contribution at home was more important than the money an outside job would bring. "A house without anyone in it is just another empty place," Millie told her spouse.

It seems ironic. So many invest so much in redecorating and remodeling a home to suit individual lifestyles, then leave it essentially deserted. Husband and wife work uptown while children occupy the homes of friends and neighbors.

Our first major investment after we were married was a 10' x 50' pink trailer house. It became our "nest"—the place where we brought our first two "fledglings" after they were born and brought them up to school age. It was where I worked and my husband "lighted" after a day on the job. Small as it was, I did my utmost to make it a welcoming place, to make our home life worthwhile.

Later, we moved to another community, into a much larger place, a 70 year old three-story structure with lots of broken plaster and possibilities. After remodeling for nearly seven years, our efforts are paying off. My husband and I have spent hundreds of hours in back-breaking labor, tearing out walls, chopping down musty plaster, hauling the entrails of our house to the city dump. Now after rebuilding, sheet-rocking, painting, papering, paneling, carpeting, our home is nearly complete.

It is even more difficult now for me to think of leaving my dream home for office space uptown!

We seem to have lost sight of the fact that a most important accomplishment of woman involves making her family feel truly cherished. As wives and parents, we must demonstrate through love to those in our care that the world is a good place.

From infancy on, children require love, enormous amounts of it. Writing in the *Reader's Digest*, Ashley Montagu cites examples which show that love is probably the most essential ingredient in a newborn's life. "We now know from the observations of a number of physicians and investigators that love is an essential part of the nourishment of every baby and that unless he is loved he will not develop as a healthy organism—psychologically, spiritually or physically. Even though he is physically well nurtured, he may nevertheless waste away and die."

This simple fact of life was not understood during the first two decades of this century; consequently, many babies perished. In the sterile climate of foundling homes babies succumbed by the dozens. Doctors realize now that this occurred because they were denied the physical warmth and cuddling that the human infant *requires* in order to desire living in this world.

Love! So basic that if we don't have it we die. How can we ever lose sight of this fact of life? Yet we have. And basically, I think, this is what is the matter with us, with our American nation. We are in the process of forgetting how to love.

Repeated assurances of parental love are essential to all children. These expressions of love afford the intimacy that babies must have in order to grow into healthy human beings, emotionally and spiritually unscarred. As parents, we can express our love in many ways—through diaper changes and nightly prayers, during feeding, chitchat after a nap, or warm cuddling before bedtime.

How well I remember my newborn's first bath. How wobbly his head seemed! How slippery his little body! He felt so fragile that I trembled as I lowered him into the water. What a tremendous responsibility, keeping this tiny human being clean, clothed, loved. Soon he was smiling—although experts claim that he was much too young to do so. While in the water, his newborn face reflected absolute contentment, and he cried only after I removed him from the warmth of his little tub.

Those early beginnings of love, so precious in retrospect, I recognize now as an actual investment—deposits made to my child's bank of emotional security. But . . . way back then, when my babies were young, there were too many distractions, too many things to be bought, too many glowing opportunities—things to take the place of warm, loving attachments.

Once again, the grass on the other side of the fence looked greener, and one morning, almost against my will, I turned to the "help wanted" section of the morning paper. I surveyed the job possibilities: legal secretary, teacher's aid, *women's editor for a small daily* . . . .

One year later I quit that job, too. It was one of the hardest things I had had to do in a long time. I quit, not because I was unhappy with my work; on the contrary, I quit because I liked it so much—more in fact than any job I had ever held.

Having a job meant being away from home; it meant having coffee breaks with grown-ups instead of milk and crackers with my chatterbox four year old. It meant interviewing prestigious political personalities and seeing my byline in the paper almost every night.

Yet it also meant frequent TV dinners instead of the homecooked variety. It meant canned soup, instead of the kind that simmers all morning on the stove, lending a special aroma to the kitchen. It meant store-bought bread instead of home-baked. It meant dropping my four year old off at the day care center at 9:00 a.m. and picking her up again around 4:00 p.m.

It meant falling asleep in the chair at 8:00 p.m. and being too tired to trudge up the stairs to tuck the children into bed or to hear their prayers. Having a job spelled death to the intimacy I had previously shared with my husband, and the long, leisurely chats before sleep. The warm physical relationship we had enjoyed together was of the past. I was always much too tired.

I had become very independent, even aggressive, and was growing to expect those luxuries that my extra paycheck afforded. I no longer thought it essential, now that I was a breadwinner too, to discuss major purchases which before had been decided upon by both my husband and myself. We quarreled frequently over money and the checkbook was much harder to balance than it had been when we had to manage it ever so carefully.

Having a job was an exciting break in the confining routine of raising a family; yet, fortunately, I could see that my job was becoming far too exciting. It was becoming even more important to me than my family. My priorities had become confused.

I needed to remind myself of the temporariness of the moment:

Lord, help me to appreciate the here-and-nowness of my life. Let me savor the soft falling of snow on the roof, a cup of coffee, my open fire. Time is so fleeting. Let me enjoy this child on my lap, the sound of my own voice reading a familiar story. Remove my need for worldly goods and accomplishments—plaques, titles, glory. Lord, grant me a heart grateful for the commonplace!

3
NESTBUILDER:
Occupational Hazards

Self-esteem is an essential ingredient to happy, Christlike living. Dr. James Dobson has said, "If I could write a prescription for the women of the world, it would provide each of them with a healthy dose of self-esteem and personal worth (taken three times a day)."

Truly women, especially of the profession Nestbuilder, need a fully developed inner sense of self-worth. The conviction that we are vital, contributing members of society can keep us on the job when the glitter of the world outside tempts us to throw in our aprons and join the sorority of working mothers and wives.

Children, too, search for that sense of self that makes them feel special. The other evening after I had tucked my little girl, Kirsten, into bed and listened to her rather lengthy prayers with all her "God blesses" (Grandma, Grandpa, cousins, aunts and uncles), I turned to go back downstairs.

She called after me, "Wait, Mommie. I forgot to bless someone."

"Who is that?" I wondered.

"*Me*," she said with a grin.

When I go about my housework, sometimes I sneeze. Nobody is around usually, so I have gotten into the habit of saying, "God bless me!"

Peculiar? Perhaps—yet I think my motives for so doing are psychologically sound and in accordance with God's will. I am, after all, a *child of God*. Doesn't it then logically follow that I deserve my own support, loyalty and friendship? For our mental health's sake, our own loving concern becomes essential.

During my coffee break at home, more often than not, I am a coffee klatch of one. Without self-communication, without a long-lasting friendship with myself, I would truly be a lonely person, overly dependent on my family for feelings of support and fulfillment.

Self-love is not sin. Think about it: Christ commanded that we love our neighbors as ourselves—not more than, but "as." If we do not believe in our own inherent worth, we cannot accept and love others as Christ meant for us to love them. I cannot shower someone with more love than is mine to give. I can only give as much as I have. For example, if I love myself, say half the time, how can I love my family all the time? I haven't got that much love to give.

Unfortunately, many of us have a hard time loving the person that is *me*. We have the feeling that love for self represents a form of sin. Lest we become self-centered, self-seeking and selfish, many of us try to steer clear of self-love altogether. Christ did warn against a certain kind of self-love. Self-indulgence which leads to greediness, self-centeredness and glorification of self at another's expense He soundly denounced.

Yet, there is a wholesome, creative, self-liberating kind of love for self that proclaims, "I *am* because God made me, and thus, I am worthy of my own friendship." As a child of the Heavenly Father, I need no justification for my existence other than that God has made me.

My worldly accomplishments will not buy my time here on earth. My good works, the money I make, the children I have, the books I write—while all these are worthwhile and make life meaningful—do not justify my existence. God has already done that for me through Jesus Christ.

Since I have become my own best friend, I am the understanding parent to the troubled child that exists within me. All the kind, loving attention I formerly reserved for others—children, spouse and friends—I now shower on myself, too. I have learned when to make demands of myself, when to let up, when to comfort. As I get to know myself better, I am more aware of my full God-given potential as a human being. I know when I can safely push my internal gas pedal all the way to the floor.

My friendship with self is an enormous boon in my life. I am my own cheerleader, so to speak. Writing in *How To Be Your Own Best Friend*, Drs. Mildred Newman and Bernard Berkowitz say, "You must learn to talk to yourself. You need to explain things, to reassure yourself.'' Establish an ongoing dialogue with yourself. This can help you through all kinds of tough situations.

Becoming one's own best friend involves dwelling on the positive aspects of one's life. Successes, good behavior, triumphs of a personal nature—think on these! Stay your mind against past mistakes, failures and humiliations.

Try new things! You will find that with your own loving support almost anything is possible. For example, I had convinced myself that I could not talk before a large audience. When our local Lion's Club program chairman asked me to give a talk, I almost refused. Then I realized my fear stemmed from an unrealistic desire to give them a perfect performance. Ultimately I decided to do it. I would do the thing I feared practically more than anything else!

I practiced and prayed, prayed and practiced. And when I stood before that group of perhaps forty men, a wonderful assurance came over me. I delivered my speech without faltering, holding their rapt attention for twenty minutes. When I had finished, they gave me a hearty round of applause! No sound ever held such sweetness for me.

Self-hate *is* sin. Many Christians unwittingly engage in self-hating devices because we are traditionally idealistic, particularly in the realm of our own conduct. It seems the more we elevate goals for self, the more prone we become to self-hate should we not live up to these exalted ideals. When choosing a destination for self, we must learn to ask: Is this a realistic possibility for me? With my God-given abilities can I possibly achieve this? Or am I merely hoping to be something that I am not?

A man barely five feet tall should not aspire to become a pro basketball player. Certainly he can play on his own court, challenge his son or daughter in games of rough and tumble. But aspiring to stardom in this realm would be foolish. We must rid ourselves of illusions, carry-overs from childhood, dreams out of line with the role God has in mind for us in His world, without refusing to set viable goals which we *can* achieve.

Before I became my own best friend, I engaged in a lot of self-destructive habits. If I felt that I had said or done something wrong, I would literally make myself ill worrying about it. If I thought I might have hurt another's feelings, my regret and remorse would become so overpowering that I would torture myself with recriminations totally out of proportion to my misdeed, real or imagined. "I can't stand myself," I would say. I had set myself up as God, serving as my own judge and jury.

An ancient philosopher said, "If one is cruel to himself, how can we expect him to be compassionate with others?" I now realize that Christ's forgiving love begins through the administration of compassion to the person that is myself.

Self-hate often rears its ugly head in the form of comments such as, "I'm no good" or "I'm stupid." Remarks such as, "I can't ever do anything right" usually surface just before we are about to accomplish something truly constructive and worthwhile. Fearing our own failure, we rush to condemn self, even before we perform (in order to beat possible critics to the punch!). Sometimes these negative thoughts can be traced back to childhood. Often they represent verbal playbacks, sometimes word for word, spoken by unfeeling parents.

Self-hate shows itself, too, in the form of self-derisive fantasies—picturing oneself naked before the world, so to speak. We might visualize ourselves alone and forsaken, without a friend. At other times we might engage in vindictive self-criticism for the ostensible purpose of self-improvement. The real goal, masochistic self-flagellation, however, is not so healthy.

Enormous energy is wasted in the service of self-hate. Denigrating oneself can be paralyzing; it severely reduces our Christian potential. Self-hate wipes out creativity and eliminates accomplishment.

In his book, *Compassion and Self-Hate*, Dr. Theodore Isaac Rubin writes about one of his patients, an architect. He was a highly credited member of his trade, yet he could not tolerate criticism of his work. His standards for himself were so out of reach that he became almost apoplectic in his struggle to live up to internal disciplines.

Eventually, as this man's fears grew entirely out of proportion, he was forced to quit the work that meant so much to him. His unreasonable self-demands seemed inexplicable until the patient, during one session, revealed a tyrannical father who expected from his son nothing less than perfection. Only after he realized that being human barred him from the perfection that is God's did he achieve inner peace.

Without self-liberating love, sometimes a person will engage in an ongoing conspiracy against self. Many times such a person will hide behind a facade of dependency, a front designed to hide true self and frequently enormous human potential. I know a woman who seemed unable to do anything. The simplest decision was impossible for her. Sewing, cooking, dealing with her children seemed beyond her ken.

She was addicted to her psychiatrist who kept her sedated much of the time. One day she discovered her own power potential through Jesus Christ. After flushing her array of pink and orange tranquilizers down the toilet, she went to work. Utilizing hidden, God-given talents, she far surpasses all of us who in the past waited on her!

As my own best friend, the offspring of the Divine Architect, I am much more than the psychiatrists say I am. Not an instinct-manipulated puppet or a stimulus-response machine, I am the *child of God*.

My heritage grants my existence special value. I am a free, willing entity. It is my sacred responsibility to discern right from wrong, good from evil. The New and Old Testaments provide my life's guidelines. To the best of my ability I try to live up to the commands therein. This makes me a unique being in a secular age. And, as a child of God, I have more power potential than my sisters divorced from His wisdom and loving vitality.

We must come to terms with the forces that war within. Self-depreciation can be combated only through the loving power of Jesus Christ. We must be reborn in Him. Then enlist the Holy Spirit. In this battle we need the full armour of God. Perfection is not a human achievement. We can become good, great even, but perfection is Christ's exclusively. Self-castigating behavior goes contrary to Christ's example. So, develop a compassionate regard for self. Learn to view yourself in God's perspective. Try to get outside of your own self-condemnation; be objective, if you can.

Christ possessed self-integrating respect for the Being He was. He did not condemn or condone; Christ had compassion. A compassion so all-encompassing that it included those who nailed His hands to the cross and left Him to die. Never did He minimize His mission on this earth by self-effacement. Instead, Christ displayed a healthy self-esteem in all dealings with Himself as well as with the world. His character was not a passive abstraction, but a living, practical reality. Christ's total Person includes love for others as well as self. Jesus had to be *His* own best friend in order to endure the agony He suffered on the cross for you and me.

Christ's life on earth provides our example. If God considers me worthy of justification, how can I possibly accept an alternative contrary to the self-love concept Christ has ordained?

My self-love, if genuine, will be evident to those around me. My inner security will wrap itself around my family, cloaking those in my care in love and acceptance.

Children absorb attitudes by osmosis. If I, as a

parent, transmit my belief of self worth, they will absorb this attitude toward me and toward themselves as well. My healthy self-appreciation will teach them respect—for me as a person and for themselves.

4
MARRIAGE:
Basic Fibre Of The Nest

Before Christ's arrival on earth, women were treated shabbily. A pagan Roman husband might divorce his bride on the slightest pretext, casting her adrift without a penny. Under ancient Roman statutes, she had no recourse in a court of law.

Happily, Christianity changed all that. God liberated women through Jesus Christ—yes, even women of my calling, wives, mothers, keepers of the nest. Under the New Testament laws, woman became esteemed. Laws were passed that recognized her childbearing and nurturing responsibilities, and wayward husbands were made accountable to wives and children.

Today, the American Christian home reflects those early values. In spite of the moral revolution, thousands of American husbands and wives esteem one another. When each possesses a mutual respect for the other and for God's laws, there is nothing that can cast their relationship asunder.

Just how important this loyal devotion to each other is to the children of the union was brought home to us the other evening when our youngest clambered into our laps as we watched television together. Earlier that evening her daddy and I had exchanged harsh words.

She looked at me with wide eyes saying, "Mama, do you love Dad?" I answered in the affirmative, puzzled, for I had forgotten our earlier clash of tempers.

Then she turned open eyes on her father asking the same question. Only after a positive response from him did she settle down to snuggle contentedly between us.

Do we realize how much children are influenced by their parents' relationship? It has been said, and I think wisely, that the best gift we can give our children is a loving, sturdy marriage grounded in faith and love of God.

The first model children have for all relationships throughout life is the one they observe between their mother and father. If that example is warm—if husband and wife are mutually concerned and supportive of one another, if they display evidence of their love by holding hands, touching, even occasionally embracing one another in the presence of their children—then youngsters will absorb a positive lesson about life and human relationships in general.

Dr. David Goodman, author of *A Parent's Guide to the Emotional Needs of Children*, writes that there is a definite relatedness between parental sexual happiness and their offsprings' emotional security. The function of sex in marriage, he says, is not limited to the purpose of procreation. Sex is for the even greater purpose of sustaining the products of our love in an atmosphere of warm emotional security.

Recent surveys reveal that Christians, in spite of their rigid, Puritanical reputation in this area, are actually more sexually responsive than their secular counterparts. Why is this? A Christian couple's relationship with Jesus Christ enhances their ability to give and receive love in every phase of their lives together, including the sexual realm.

Prudish ideas about sex are not the product of Bible truth. The Scriptures reveal sex to be a sacred part of a happy marriage. It is explicit in its approval of the intimate relationship between married persons. God is the Author of sex and nothing he has created is bad—when used as he intended. "Be fruitful and multiply" was God's first command to Adam and Eve. Even before sin came into the world, God told his children to "replenish the earth."

In Matthew 19:5, married partners are enjoined to "be one flesh." Again in Hebrews 13:4: "Marriage is honourable in all and the bed undefiled."

In Christian marriage when priorities are in order, husbands, wives and children esteem one another. Thus, everyone gains as we take on the proper perspective—God's perspective. Who would guess it? Being a sweetheart to their daddy is the most valuable thing a mother can do for her children!

Entrusted to wives is the sacred duty of keeping domestic harmony. If she is successful in winning her mate's full love, a woman's parental challenge will be much easier. From the man's point of view, having received the full devotion of his mate, the husband becomes a more willing aid in the upbringing of their children. Kids in turn tend to cooperate more fully when they realize that their parents are working together as a team.

Marriages do not spring up in blooming devotion and harmony by themselves. Creating a good marriage requires prayer, commitment, caring. A successful marriage is the result of hard work and "stick-to-it-iveness." In our grandparents' day "until death do us part" meant something. Commitment, staying power, was a commodity as thick as glue, and "for better or worse" they stuck it out! Commitment to each other, to the vows made before God, is the fibre of the strong marriage.

In our society's current process of change, traditional male/female roles and values are being altered. Years ago, women felt fulfilled at home because they were so desperately needed by the family. The preparation of meals and of clothing for the family, along with housekeeping duties, required most of the homemaker's time and much of her energy.

Today, her job is easier, yet paradoxically it is more difficult. Energies are not fully expended by home duties. Consequently, many women take their excess energies to market. But women who are divided between two callings often find themselves existing in a schizoid world. The working woman's inflexible schedule will not allow her to be all things to all people, and she often ends her day feeling divided and disloyal.

But—if women have changed, so have their men. Man, driven by competition for jobs and promotions, has frequently all but abandoned the role of husband and father. His burning desire to succeed in his job has led him to overplay his part as provider.

The result of these independent searches for fulfillment outside the home? *Emotional chaos on a grand scale.*

Human nature over the centuries has not changed, although the circumstances of our lives have been altered. Then, as now, the solution to important problems lies in Scripture. Paul, writing to the Ephesians from his prison cell in Rome, tells those ancients to "be subject to one another out of reverence for Christ."

Paul says to those harried couples of the early church, "be submissive" and adaptive as a service to the Lord. A husband now, as then, is to be the head of the wife. Paul urges wives in turn to respect and reverence their men, to venerate and esteem them, to defer to them, to praise them, love and admire them exceedingly! Would it be possible for any wife to woo as Paul commands without becoming her mate's perennial sweetheart?

Christian love toward one another is patient, kind and unconditional. If I love my husband in the Christlike tradition, I will love him regardless of his irritating habit of dropping his clothes all over the bedroom. I will think more of his steadfastness, his loyalty to his family, his love for me.

John Powell writes in his *Secret of Staying in Love,* "Love may be given either conditionally or unconditionally," yet the only kind of love which produces change is that which is unconditional. Conditional love degenerates into what he terms "pan-scale" exchanges. Under this system, both parties are expected to contribute love equally so that a balance is achieved.

"Sooner or later some tension, some pain will distract one of the pan-scale lovers, and he/she will not make his monthly payment on time." Refusing to be swindled, the other partner will remove part of his/her contribution in order to be certain that more isn't going out than is coming in. Eventually, all that is left is emotional and/or legal divorce.

This Christian writer relates the story of a husband whose love for his wife hinged on whether or not she kept her home immaculate. The wife contended, however, that she needed to feel her mate's affection unconditionally in order to have the strength to carry out his wishes.

As women, keepers of the marital flame as well as builders of the nest, we must be continually aware of our mate's need to feel loved, cherished beyond any other. If we fail to keep trying to improve our marriage, it may succumb to the epidemic of marital disease, as so many have. Even long, enduring marriages seem not to be immune to this epidemic.

A friend wrote in her Christmas letter that she and her husband were divorcing. Somehow, I felt almost angry and betrayed. To me their union represented years of experiences shared, commitment and growth for both partners. What had happened to make them change their minds after almost 20 years?

I did not feel anger at my friends personally. Instead I felt a sense of remorse over the loss and waste—the same kind of loss I feel whenever I pass through a neighboring town and see a rather elaborate cement foundation that was abandoned because inspectors pronounced it structurally unsound.

Permanence, persistence, patience in a marital relationship are fruits of a Christian involvement. Watching one's mate mature and change, while at the same time experiencing similar alterations in mind, spirit, and temperament is a benefit of the long-lasting marriage.

Divorce is so serious that the Bible does not allow it except in instances of adultery. Why is the Bible so strict, almost harsh in its pronouncement against divorce? The Bible is so against divorce because divorce hurts! Its chief victims are children. A child's happiness begins in parental love; from it flows all his/her blessings. Its lack causes much of life's early trauma.

The marital relationship is so very vital because it deeply involves everyone in the family unit—husband, wife, and precious young lives. A child's most basic security is in knowing that his parents love each other. It's even more important to him than their love for him. He feels assured of remaining part of a strong, continuing relationship when we as parents give our interpersonal relationship the priority it deserves—no, demands.

5
THE NEST:
Vacancy Forthcoming

Oftentimes we feel trapped once we are totally committed to the responsibility of nestkeeping. If we are doing a truly conscientious job, we find that home, children and husband demand most of our physical energies and emotional resources. For this reason, many young homemakers find themselves eager for escape. We desire a loftier pursuit, a job more esteemed by the world, yet one less demanding of internal resources.

A question, then, which we should answer for ourselves: *How can I have the best of both worlds? How can I do a conscientious job of nestkeeping and still have a touch of glamour all my own?*

If we have patience and perspective, fulfillment can be the sum of seemingly inconsequential acts. Viewed on a grand scale, even the most demeaning job takes on importance.

Take child-raising, for instance. What could be more servile than washing dirty diapers? There are too many tiresome, trivial duties connected with motherhood to list; yet, when viewed in perspective, the job of being mother takes on tremendous importance. What could be more prestigious in this day and age than bringing up a well-adjusted youngster, physically, mentally and emotionally unscarred, ready to deal with a difficult world?

Finding a proper balance between self and family takes some real coordinating, but outside interests are vital to our well-being, especially when we are isolated much of the time from other adults. Without interests of our own it is easy to become so caught up with family that we become a nuisance. We all know "total" mothers, pathetic women, so worried that they cannot relax for even a minute when one of their darlings is out of sight.

Then too, relief from trying chores is a crying need. My desire to get away for a breather has little or nothing to do with my personhood or fulfillment; rather it involves diversion, therapy for a wilted psyche. All of us occasionally owe ourselves some of life's pleasures. So go ahead—get a sitter and get out of the house. Get away from the noise and the demands of your family. Dress up and go uptown. Get your hair done. Buy a new outfit if you can afford it (maybe even if you can't). Have lunch with someone who is not wearing a bib!

But should we consider full-time or even part-time employment away from those we love most? I really do lap up the prestige of a job, dressing up everyday, being able to say, "Why yes, I work!" Still I don't relish punching a time clock or having to live up to another's schedule.

I have no check, true, other than the few stories I

sell or the baby-sitting I occasionally do, but there are other compensations in my line of work as nestbuilder. Small, seemingly inconsequential things, yet these are the things that give my life special flavor. A jar filled with dandelions graces my kitchen counter, delivered this morning by a gap-toothed gidget. On my refrigerator there is a note, a thoughtful gesture from a seventh grader, "Mom, I'm at Barb's. Where are you?" From time to time I discover, too, that I am needed, really needed. Like this afternoon when my teenager dragged in from school with tears burning in somber eyes. *What if I had not been there?*

Besides our children's needs, our husbands look to us for comfort and edification. Those who would rearrange our society overlook one important aspect of our humanity. Male and female are not *just* sexual opposites. They are poles apart in thinking, feeling, the adjustments made in life. This is due to inborn, God-given differences which time and circumstance cannot alter.

When a man seeks out a partner in life, he seeks more than sexual release. In Proverbs 31, the Bible tells us that if a man can find a truly good wife, she is worth more than precious gems. Her husband can trust her; she will richly satisfy his manly needs. She will not hinder him, but will help him all her life.

She is full of strength and dignity. When she speaks, her words are well chosen and kindness is the rule for everything. She watches carefully all that goes on in her household. Never is she lazy. Her children stand up and bless her, as does her husband.

A fulfilled woman? In the truest sense. Although she runs her own home-based business, she all the while keeps a close eye on family members, seeing first to their needs.

Women in Biblical times, women of the caliber described in Proverbs 31, were a great civilizing force. By creatively adapting themselves, they domesticated their males' inherent restlessness. They realized instinctively that men look to women as the stabilizing force in their lives, to amplify their part in society.

God has designed woman to complement, not compete with her mate. There is nothing in the male body to dictate any settled pattern of life. Female sexuality is by nature cyclic and rhythmic, geared ultimately to reproduction and the subsequent nurturing of offspring. The brief performance of the male is counter-balanced by the full-blown, unfolding process of childbirth for the woman. When a man loves deeply he puts aside his nomadic tendencies, becoming involved in the nurturing of the offspring that he has helped to conceive.

Mothers and wives whose better judgment has been swayed by the Pied Pipers of fulfillment-at-any-cost are bound for disappointment. Priorities askew, these modern-day Delilahs relegate husband and children to the category of second-class citizens. They seek instead glorification of a more personal nature.

Isn't there some middle ground? Can't fulfillment be a journey as well as an exalted destination? I think so. "For everything there is a season," the Scriptures tell us. There is a time and a place for everything under the sun. A time to marry, a time to bear children, a time to nurture and love those children (Ecclesiastes 3).

As we learn to adapt to a husband, we at the same time teach our children to get along more and more without us. As they need us less and less, we can squeeze in a hobby or special interest of our own. Eventually when the nest empties, when we are established firmly in our husband's heart (having made ourselves indispensable to his happiness), we can at last focus our energies on our private little niche.

It seemed horribly pretentious at first, but I started to write. Secretly, of course. At that time we lived in the trailer house in a tiny, isolated mining community in the Nevada desert. I enrolled in a writing course advertised in a magazine, yet I never seemed to find time to complete the assignments.

Writing afforded the escape I needed so desperately, although finding time for it was never easy. Once when I dared to mail my maternal grandmother one of my poems, she wrote back a scolding letter, "I hope you're not writing and neglecting those precious children!"

Well, I wasn't neglecting my precious children and I was busy, far too busy, but somehow I stuck with my hobby. My beginnings as a writer were small, but I managed to read or to squeeze in time for my writing nearly every day.

At first I jotted off poems or children's stories;

later I wrote short-shorts with *very* clipped endings. After all, there were always laundry and cooking and screaming babies to be taken care of. I knew I wasn't bound for the bestseller list, right away anyway, for those heartless editors rejected one attempt after another.

Somewhere I read that writers need to read a lot, so I read a lot. The more I read, it seemed, the more dogmatic I became in my opinions about the world's problems. If only "they" would listen to me I could solve everything! My speciality became letters-to-the-editor, which I bashfully failed to sign at first. Later I gained the courage of my convictions and dashed one off almost every day, signed! I sent in column ideas to the local paper, which they turned down on a regular basis.

No writing space, a dire shortage of writing time, two young children with another on the way—and a husband who kept saying, "Quit wasting your time!" kept me from becoming the serious writer I had hoped to become. *I am not meant to write,* I concluded one forlorn day when the mailman delivered yet another manila envelope with yet another form rejection slip. I quit writing. I folded up my dream and put it away along with my Smith-Corona.

Soon after that we moved to the small southern Oregon community of Lakeview. Up to that time I had never laid eyes on another freelance writer, a person with genuine literary aspirations like my own. And until then I had felt almost certain that I would never, ever encounter such a person, at least not in the flesh. But there was an active writer's group in town.

Although I had long since abandoned all writing hopes, I decided to attend one of their meetings. *A good way to get acquainted,* I reasoned. At that first meeting I met not one, but a half dozen, genuine, flesh-and-blood freelance writers. They were a diversified group. One member, a housewife like myself, had that week received a check for $250 for a short piece sold to a national market.

Another struggled to write mysteries. Some specialized in the Christian market. When they read their pieces aloud for criticism, their work seemed professional. And the comments offered by the individual members proved so penetrating and helpful that one of the writers claimed she had sold several of her rejected pieces after making the changes suggested by the group. I was impressed.

I dug out my Smith-Corona. Setting up a writing table in the basement, I started again. Although the basement was dark, dank and frequented by huge, unfriendly spiders, it was a spot where I could be alone, for a few minutes at least.

I was still unsuccessful. My rejected submissions found my address in Oregon as easily as they had in Nevada. Yet now I had encouragement. I had the support of other writers, sometimes successful ones—who at one time had felt every bit as hopeless about ever selling their work as I did.

I reworked my old stories, submitting them to smaller markets. Still, my next 99 submissions were flatly rejected. I was beginning to wonder if my husband wasn't right after all. *Was* I wasting my time?

Then, one sunny September day, the mailman deposited in my mailbox not a familiar manila envelope—but a check. A check for $10 from Standard Publishing Company. *Today's Christian Mother* was actually paying me for something I had written!

Thinking that *now* all doors were open to me, I dug out all my old rejects, polishing them up. I mailed them off with a new air of confidence. It was two years, however, before I sold another piece.

Since then I have sold nearly 50 pieces. One of them had been around nearly ten years, being revised and resubmitted again and again.

This year, with all my children in school, I have time to really do the writing I have longed to do for some time. The grandmother who warned against my writing and neglecting my family now encourages me. She buys me stamps and tells people, "She'll bring honor to the family!"

And my husband has stopped making fun of my efforts. He set up a writing corner for me in our living room and bought me a new electric typewriter for my birthday.

My hobby renews my sense of self, and is one of the few occupations which blend with a busy family life. Try if you can to choose a diversion for your interests that can be pursued while the kids are growing up and underfoot, such as painting, writing, editing, volunteer work. Pursue your interests as much as your schedule will allow, even if only on a piecemeal basis at first. Then, expand gradually as free time grows.

For many of us homemakers, fulfillment is tied closely with family. Self-actualization becomes the by-product of involvement with those we love most. American women actually have the best of all worlds. We are faced with more opportunities than any other women in the history of the world.

But don't let all these choices be your undoing! Stay your focus on your family and your relationship with Jesus Christ. And only then grow into an interest that will keep you happily busy, and perhaps even financially independent, the remainder of your life.

It is true that there are times when, no matter how we try to organize our time, most of it is taken up in unglamourous chores. Yet, even during those hectic years there is a certain amount of freedom. On call 24 hours a day, seven days a week, I still have more free time than my husband who must put in a 40 hour shift every week.

Even during my hectic schedule with little ones underfoot, it is possible to shoe-horn in time for special interests. Taking my cue from the Bible's own liberated lady in Proverbs 31, I have come to realize that fulfillment really is the sum total of seemingly inconsequential acts.

6
GRACIOUSNESS:
Mortar Of The Nest

In the bustle of everyday life there is often a tendency to put courtesy aside. In our haste, rudeness can too easily become a way of life. It will show on our scowling faces, in our gestures of impatience, in our constant flurry to get things done. The homemaker, then, who has the ability to create an ambiance of gracious concern for her family, can provide a refreshing contrast to what the family may encounter outside the home.

Getting along with those in our community is a gift to be prized greatly, too. The ability to see another's point of view, to compromise, and to practice the Golden Rule is truly a valuable personality asset for builders of the nest.

For some, graciousness seems to be inborn, instinctive. Others of us have to really work at it. A few years ago when living in the southwest hills of Portland, Oregon, I was painting the porch of my small apartment one late August afternoon. A band of boys who were playing cops and robbers among the trees and bushes of the neighborhood stopped to see what I was doing. Their leader, a youngster of perhaps ten with curly, carrot-colored hair, stood with his hands in his jeans pockets surveying me. Bolder than the rest, he emerged from the group to observe more closely.

"Ma'am," he addressed me politely, "did you know that you have green paint on your face?"

Before I could reply he quickly mollified his observation with, "But on you it looks good!"

He flashed me a gypsy grin; then, as swiftly as they had appeared, the entire force was gone, again restoring law and order in the blackberry forest.

I am almost certain that young man will have an easy time in this world! His natural tact and good-will are bound to win him friends, open many doors, procure many opportunities.

Graciousness! What is this quality that makes even the plainest woman seem beautiful? That transforms the most everyday person into a being of nobility?

My dictionary offers several explanations of this pleasing trait. The person who possesses graciousness is marked by the Christian qualities of kindness and courtesy. He or she is graceful with tact and delicacy. The gracious person is a delight to be with; he puts one at ease. Graciousness involves giving of oneself. Graciousness is reciprocal; it gives and receives with equal poise. It says thank you, replenishing the giver with compliments from the heart. It is the white lie that softens hurtful truth.

It accepts defeat without sourness, winning without haughtiness. Graciousness pays its own

·way, and in giving it does so anonymously, turning its gaze to avoid the eyes of the receiver.

Graciousness is Eleanor Roosevelt foregoing self-pity on the event of her husband's death, comforting and consoling Harry Truman without mention of her own great loss. It is my neighbor reaching over the fence to pull my weeds. It is Rose Kennedy's concern for Nixon's mother after the Kennedy-Nixon debates in 1960. It is my son helping his aged great-grandmother out of the car and into her house.

How often are we as homemakers present in body only, offering no real substance of our spirit, even to those closest to us? How often have we stared blankly into our child's eyes without hearing a word that was spoken? When we are so preoccupied, we cannot communicate with one another.

The simple art of being gracious can rescue a marriage on the brink of divorce. A good friend told me recently about her marital near-disaster. She and her mate would arrive home from their jobs in the evening, each emotionally drained from the day's activities.

"We fell into a routine of grouching and picking at one another," she said. When she realized that they had gotten into a habit of rudeness, she vowed to change. "We wouldn't have dreamed of treating a guest like we were treating one another!"

After prayer, after invoking the aid of the Holy Spirit, it was easier to make it a point to greet her husband at the door with a smile and a kiss. "The change in our lives has been miraculous," she told me. "We've become like honeymooners again!"

OCCUPATION: NESTBUILDER

Kindness, like a pebble rippling through a still pond, creates a series of concentric rings, a series of happenings which radiate into the universe, penetrating the hard shell of hate and indifference.

Graciousness demands of us what is best in our human potential. It draws from us a vital investment and a fresh reinvestment every day of our lives. Is this why a truly gracious person is never a bore, why we seek his or her presence?

I have in mind a friend. He is interested in others and lets it show. Through his conversation he relays compassion, an attitude of genuine caring. Many of us hold back, fearful of intimacy, of expressing our deepest feelings, afraid of getting involved, reluctant to expose too much of ourselves.

My friend puts me at ease by creating an atmosphere of acceptance. In his presence I am not on stage, so to speak. I do not feel pressed to be witty, well-read—or even cheerful, when I feel otherwise. He accepts my moods as he welcomes the variances in the weather. If I go to him with a problem, he is supportive. Whenever I am perplexed about something he pulls a similar problem out of his hat of memories. He has had trouble too, or knows someone who has suffered similarly. Always he encourages. I come away feeling that I have been heard and understood, counseled wisely. Luckily this friend is my life's companion, my husband.

Another friend who is especially easy to be with has the gift of humor, a capacity to blitz hypocrisy with her gentle wit. While she takes herself seriously, she is never so stuffy that she cannot laugh at herself. With emotion bordering on glee she dredges up her own snags and frailties, parading them before me in order to make me feel better about my own. I relax in her presence because she is so far from perfect—human and humane, warm and funny.

Generally she is agreeable, but this is not to say that she holds no firm opinions. I have seen her clench her fist and pound her table in order to emphasize a point in which she believes. Yet she has the knack of stating her feelings in such a way that she herself doesn't become disagreeable.

To exist in grace brings inner harmony translated to others through outward peace. Still, *how* do they work such social magic? How is all this to be achieved in a frantically busy world, especially by so many of us entrained with the multiple demands of job, spouse, children? How can I be gracious when I am over-tired, bogged down in responsibilities that drain and deplete my store of goodwill?

Are some born prepossessed of such grace, while others of us are doomed to a life of social trial-and-error? I think not. The art of being truly gracious can be achieved by even the most ordinary of us. First, though, certain qualities must be cultivated and practiced so that being graciously civil becomes second nature.

While graciousness, in my estimation, cannot be taught, it can be caught. If you have a friend who deftly incorporates the social graces in his or her relationships with others, study his or her habits. Imitate and incorporate. Adapt and adopt into your own unique style those qualities that make your friend so easy to like. If your friend notices you are doing this, he or she is certain to be flattered.

Thoreau gave us the answer, at least in part, to the art of being gracious. "Simplify," he advised. Simplify. Cut out all but the most essential doings. Keep a calendar of events that bring you pleasure. If some activity is especially trying, get out of it if you possibly can. You cannot escape all responsibility, join a convent or a monastery, but you can strive for a balance between yourself and your obligations to others.

As Anne Morrow Lindberg points out in *A Gift From the Sea,* the most exhausting thing in life is insincerity. If graciousness is to be more than a show of superficial politeness it must come from the heart.

The protocol of graciousness requires that we admit errors, rectify mistakes. Being gracious means having to say "I'm sorry," not once but time and time again. Its rules of order demand that we bear no grudges but be quick to forgive.

An example of this caring quality is found in the old Mary Tyler Moore shows which I sometimes watch with my children after school. Graciousness is brought to life by the charming Mary Richards, who—through her underlying patience with the skinflint Ted Baxter, her sympathy with the dizzy Georgette, her unfailing tolerance of the foibles of Sue Ann Nevins and Lou Grant, her unmatched forbearance in relationships with eccentric apartment-mates, Phyllis and Rhoda—makes me wish I had a friend like her!

The opposites of graciousness thrive—gruffness,

sharpness, abruptness—especially in our busy cities where so many are concerned more about making money and acquiring things than establishing bonds with other human beings. On our freeways especially, wouldn't it be wonderful if all those drivers could be given a heaping dose of graciousness?

Graciousness can be a characteristic of the rich and powerful, or a quality of the poor. While fame, position and wealth may be accidental, the world's true aristocracy is characterized by its spirit of graciousness. Graciousness is an accumulation of little kindnesses and concessions. It is distinctly the virtue of many Christians, yet its practitioners may be found among all the great religions of the world which teach their followers the whole law of doing good and returning good for evil.

A revival of the spirit of graciousness could have a truly revolutionary impact on our families as well as our world, for essentially graciousness is love in action, in all the various manifestations with which we choose to bring it to life!

7
THE NEST:
Clutter-Free

From the doghouse to the dining room, everything was in chaos. No matter how hard I tried, my living room never seemed to possess that homey "lived-in" look that I so prized. Instead, it always resembled the aftermath of Hurricane Hilda.

When my husband was at work his boots were on his feet. Otherwise, uprooted and unlaced, they flanked the right side of his recliner. Unless, of course, I picked them up. When the kids were home from school I found it impossible to keep up. My kitchen was always a shambles, with half-eaten sandwiches, empty milk cartons, an open peanut butter jar leering from the table.

The linoleum was constantly sticky and gritty with sand and dirt from their trips to the lake. Seeds were strewn about from their hamster's overflowing cage, intermixed with spilled lemonade. When I stubbed my toe on Boliver's bone and cried out bitterly, it was more from emotional pain than physical.

Upstairs in the children's bedrooms I discovered a host of unmade beds and chests-of-drawers agape, spewing forth their untidy insides. Comic books, gum wrappers and dirty socks accented the mood of disarray and my feeling of utter hopelessness.

Clutter invites more clutter. "This place is a mess," my twelve year old son said as he kicked his way through the rubble into the bathroom. No sooner had the words escaped his lips than he dropped his candy bar wrapper into the midst of it all.

Somewhere along the line my kids had failed to make the transition from infantile dependence to picking up after themselves. When I finally realized that my system (or non-system) of keeping house was self-punishing, I revolted. As a domestic engineer I was a flop. My self-punishing, masochistic methods had left me exhausted and angry.

Part of the reason I never got through with all those distasteful tasks was because I had never learned what every executive knows—how to delegate authority. Children (and husbands, too) must wake up to the fact that at least partial responsibility for maintaining an orderly home is theirs. In my homemaking frenzy, I was trying to do everything myself. Although there was some ego gratification in being the sole member of the fighting force, the results were chaotic.

No wonder I was a psychological mess—filled with self-hate, repressed anger and fantasies of adequacy. I was working overtime, slaving day after day, without ever making any real headway, and without any gratitude from husband or children.

Today I have *detente* with household litter. I have devised a philosophy of housekeeping that employs imagination and wit. By calling on my family's sense of fair play, by organizing in my own casual manner, we have at last achieved some semblance of order in our lives.

In one corner of our living room I have an oversized litter depository, a wicker basket with a lid which holds back issues of magazines which normal people discard, but which I like to store for future possible reference. By the fireplace there is an old copper kettle in which I store newspapers. Another basket is for library books, and an old apple crate contains the records that used to be randomly placed about the room.

Still another point of my regime involves maintaining a peaceful home life without becoming an overt nag. Taped to the bathroom mirror (where my teenagers spend a large portion of their day) is their call of duty. "Have you made your bed today? How long has it been since you dusted and vacuumed your room? Is the hamster cage tidy? Are your clothes picked up? Are your drawers closed?"

Although written notices are easy to ignore, they serve as reinforcements to the verbal commands and inspection tours.

Another part of my newly-discovered philosophy of housekeeping involves a sort of glorified sweeping under the rug plan, so at least the house looks presentable—even when under the surface it may not be.

It takes only a few minutes before I go to bed to

make a swoosh through all the rooms, chuck all the dirty dishes into the dishwasher, swish off the countertop, pick up books, papers, apple cores, straighten the living room, give the bathroom a swipe, put all soiled towels into the clothes hamper. Anything in sight I toss into a closet. (It is far less painful psychologically to straighten a closet than a whole room.)

No dusting. No vacuuming. Just picking up. Getting up the next morning is a pleasure. It at least looks peaceful.

Some of those tiresome chores have been distributed to other family members. Our son is assigned the upstairs bathroom for two weeks, a daughter the refrigerator one week, another week the ironing. My youngest keeps her toys picked up and makes her own bed. If these jobs are not done there is no television or entertainment until they are completed.

The shrew in me surfaces every so often. I have had to get tough, making demands and expecting them to be met. Self-responsibility, learning to make demands of oneself, is part of growing up. When they leave home my children will have to do these things for themselves anyway. And children who are slobs tend to develop into ungrateful, sloppy adults.

Being *family* involves helpful reciprocation. God has a better plan for my life than being a mere domestic slave. Household drudge or woman of dignity? The decision is ours.

Since I took the giant step toward a Socratic approach to keeping house, I have time for myself. I find I like myself and my children better, that my career as wife and mother has become far more satisfying. Our goal of "homey and comfortable" has at last become reality, now that my crusade against household pollution involves my entire family.

8
THE NEST:
Home Mission Field

The New Testament provides little information concerning the home into which Jesus was born and grew to manhood. Yet we can speculate that a gracious simplicity reigned, along with a rare quality of love. It was Mary as keeper of that Hebrew nest who established the tone of His early life. Mary focused her undivided energies on those she loved, fostering in her son the qualities that He would need to carry out His lifework. As overseer of the young Saviour, her name has lived for many centuries—proving once again that the hand that rocks the cradle rules the world!

Have you noticed? A truly Christian home emotes a genuine feeling of peace and security. Therefore, bringing the love of Jesus Christ into our family's midst becomes a vital function of every wife and mother.

No matter how prayerful we are on Sundays, no matter how much we give to missions around the world in our weekly offerings, if our own personal ministry at home is out of line with Christ and His teachings, we are not living up to our full Christian potential. If our home life reflects little or nothing of what we learn in church and Sunday School, our need for Christ at home must be our prime concern.

Slowly I am learning through experiences both personal and vicarious what it means to be a missionary in my own home. Mothers and wives, it seems, fall easily into the habit of nagging. We send our children to Sunday School while we wheedle and scold husbands into attending worship service with us, or into joining the church. In many homes this constitutes the beginning and the end of spiritual leadership at home. No wonder there are so few converts!

A friend, concerned about her husband's lack of religious commitment, almost drove her spouse insane with her constant harping on the subject. No matter how she pleaded and cajoled, her spouse refused to attend even one service with her. Many women face similar problems. Just how do you deal with a man's stubborn disinclination to have anything to do with your faith?

Many women fail in their mission to bring their husbands into the love of Christ because they go about it with so little understanding. A man needs to feel that he is the family leader. He needs to be the guide, protector and provider. He must earn the living, meet his family's essential needs, and do so independently without the aid of others.

A man likes to think of himself as the family's good shepherd, keeping his loved ones from danger, harm or want. Generally the husband doesn't want his wife to share his masculine burdens or to deliberately step over into his role. A man usually prefers that his wife devote herself fully to making a success of her career in the home.

Herein lies the key. When we set ourselves up as our husband's spiritual caretaker, he is bound to rebel. We are on his turf; we are taking over his role as leader of the family. Naturally he won't like it. But most men *do* want their wives to be the conscience in their lives. Being a man's conscience, however, does not include acting as his personal saviour. It is not a wife's job to convert her husband, but to love him. It is the wife's mission to help make her husband happy. Making him good is God's responsibility!

In most of our lives Jesus works gradually. If a wife remains lovingly loyal, if she maintains a spiritual example and lives up to her Christian calling as she quietly goes about her business, her husband is likely to be far more impressed than if she constantly badgers him. If she remains patient and kind, chances are that eventually she will win him over. Our mission at home is a quiet one.

But forcing the issue, arguing constantly about religion, promoting and nagging will only sour him. One man I know ultimately turned completely away, rejected his wife and children, simply because she would give him no peace.

We should not make the mistake of totaling out our marriage to make a convert of our husband. Instead, turn him over to Christ. Pray for him. Love him absolutely, the way he is. And in the fullness of

OCCUPATION: NESTBUILDER

God's time . . . .

Now, just how can we as busy keepers of the nest maintain focus on Christ and His teachings? How best can we relay His message of love to those dearest to us? How can we be certain that our children will understand life's absolutes? How can we help them carry out the "thou shalt nots" of the Bible as well as the more subtle "thou shalts"? How can I as nestbuilder, win my family to Christ, and just as importantly, stay their focus on His love and principles every day of the week?

Church and Sunday School attendance, while important, are not enough. We must bring Christ home with us. Usually it is wives and mothers who must kindle the spiritual flame and keep it burning on a day-to-day basis. A mother's mission is to set the pace.

"When the mother of the family forgets God, so does the rest of the family," reads a Navaho proverb. As stewards of Christ's love, the most important duty we women have is to bring God and His truth calmly and confidently into our family's daily lives. In our hands rests the privilege and responsibility of leading children and sometimes husbands in the knowledge and love of God.

First, our homes must reflect our Christianity. I take pride in displaying evidence of my faith—a large picture of Christ, and a prominently placed plaque, "As for me and my house, we will serve the Lord." These are reminders to family members and guests that our lives should be centered on Christ.

Home should be a place to which family members

turn for love and shelter. From the cradle onward, mothers relay the love of God through their vigilant care. As Lewis Sherrill said, "When the infant encounters love he encounters God." Ours is no small calling!

Christ truly needs us to set the example at home, to be exemplars of His perfect love. Christ needs *me* right where I am. My seven year old requires my reassuring presence after school. My teenagers need reassurance too, and help with homework. My husband requires my listening ear. They all need my prayers.

The little things we do for our families set the tone of our lives. Consider the simple ministry of listening to a child's prayers. Often it is a big temptation after a tiring day to send my little one off to bed by herself. Yet I know this is a mistake. Praying together with a child is a ministry we should not neglect.

Teach your children that no problem is too trivial or too large for God. He cares about us absolutely! Urge your child to take his or her heart's deepest desires to the Lord, and to wait patiently for His answer.

Ever since I was a little girl I have prayed before going to sleep. I remember especially those times when my mother would pray with me. She would kneel beside my bed, moonlight streaming through white ruffled curtains, to ask God to hear our prayers. Then she would go through the list of those dear to her, requesting God's blessing upon them.

"If anything is bothering you," she always said,

"you should tell God about it." How much that has meant to me over the years! How uncomplicated our lives would be if we always remembered to take our troubles to the Lord.

Mealtime too is a good time for family prayer. My father always asked grace before the evening meal when we were all together. In other homes, various members of the family participate in family prayer times following the meal. Thus, even the youngest family members have a chance to practice praying aloud to God.

Home should be a sanctuary, a place for renewal of our spirits. My grandmother was a widow who lived in the country several miles from town. She never learned to drive a car, so there was no way for her to get to church for Sunday services. Many women might have used this as an excuse to forget all about the specialness of Sunday, but not my grandmother. Her parlor became literally her place of worship.

When I was a little girl I spent many Sundays with her. Nanny, as we called her, would usher my big sister and myself into her parlor. There she would read to us from her Bible. Never will I forget the colorful geraniums that blossomed on her windowsill, filtering the late morning sunshine as she softly played her piano and sang our favorite hymns.

We must keep Sunday every day of the week. Doing so often calls for the extraordinary, going out of the way to show kindness or to rectify mistakes. The other afternoon a friend called to tell me about her parent/teacher conference at school. Expecting the usual pat on the back from her child's teacher, my friend was sorrily disappointed.

"Your daughter has developed quite a talent for cutting others down," the teacher told her. Disturbed, my friend at first blamed the teacher. The woman was nearly ready for retirement; maybe she was just too old. My friend rationalized that her daughter attended Sunday School every Sunday, and hadn't she just earned an award for memorizing the most verses of Scripture? *Still, a glib reciting of Bible verses means nothing if we don't apply them to our everyday living,* she thought.

When her daughter arrived home from school, my friend confronted her little girl with the teacher's unflattering comment. The child broke into tears. She and some other girls had teased another child for wearing shabby clothes.

"I'm sorry, Mommy," she told her mother. "I promise never to hurt anyone's feelings again." My friend decided, however, that real Christians do more than refrain from out-and-out mockery.

Together my friend and her daughter prayed. Requesting God's forgiveness, they also asked what they could do to help the child whose parents were evidently needy. They were led to call the youngster on the phone and invite her for dinner. The next Sunday the child attended Sunday School with them. Thus, the youngster was drawn into a circle of Christians who cared about her and her family's needs.

Christians care about others. If we don't, our knowledge of the Scriptures becomes mere hypocrisy. While it is important that we go to church to glean greater knowledge of Christ and His teachings, it is even more important for us to carry out those teachings in a practical way on a daily basis.

Missionary territory is not limited to Australia's outback, the wastelands of faraway South America, the slums of India. Our homes can be spiritual deserts as well. Wives and mothers, our missionary work begins at home! Not as preachers, but as examples.

Blessed is the woman who makes of her home an island of order and beauty, who preserves the sacredness of home life, who keeps Christ alive every day of the week. Her tasks are carried on in love and unconditional acceptance. She spreads joy, casting God's hope and light on those around her. Through her own experiences with Jesus Christ, she relays the vital reality of Christ to others—thereby transforming herself and her family into stewards of Christ's love.

9
FLEDGLINGS:
Dignity In Small Packages

Nestbuilding wouldn't be so vital a job if it weren't for the love needs of precious children. From babyhood, the human animal craves comfort, love, and care. When these basic drives are thwarted, the infant cries, thrashes his arms and legs, turns red in the face. If such needs are routinely denied, an infant is programmed to distrust—to feel unloved, tense and angry.

In the same vein, positive feelings of self are gleaned early. The mother who responds lovingly to her baby's cries demonstrates concern and fosters self-acceptance. Through her care, her touch, her smile, she relays a message about human love. Her concern and compassion become a backlog of positive feeling for the child. Such experiences become etched into memory, carried on through the subconscious, and become part-and-parcel of the child's developing personality.

Before a child is born, he or she feels warm and secure within the womb. After birth he endeavors to make his wants and needs understood. It becomes a parent's duty to aid in the struggle, to help the infant grow in trust, to teach the child that the world is a good place in which to be.

Excursions out of the nest, away from mother's familiar skirts, represent a hardship for many sensitive youngsters. Wise parents recognize the difficulty of early separations and enhance trust by dealing diplomatically with their children. Enormous harm can be done to a young "clinger" if separations are either too abrupt or unnecessarily prolonged.

When I was very young, perhaps nearly three years old, I was extremely timid, a clinger to my mother's skirts. My mother considered it her conscientious duty to snap me out of it, to make a joiner out of me, to get me out of her kitchen into the gregarious world of the neighborhood playground. The more she pushed, however, the more I stubbornly huddled near her, savoring the security of her familiar presence.

One day she took me into her arms and squeezed me to her ample bosom. "I'll hug you so tight! I'll never let you go," she told me. At first I regarded it as a delightful game; then I began to push away, wriggling to get free.

We both learned something of reverse psychology that morning. There were no more pleadings for me to come with her to the playground. Instead, she issued stern warnings against my leaving her side or wandering over to the nearby park. At first I was pleased. I felt wanted and secure. But soon my delight faded. I began to gaze longingly through our screen door at the forbidden park, with its swings and slides and other children. At last I longed to try my social wings.

My mother helped me into my coat and slipped on her own plaid jacket. Arm in arm, we made our way to that world of peer involvement. There must have been an expression of triumph on her face as she took her place on the park bench alongside the other mothers.

According to many child experts, parents need to be concerned with fostering a positive self-image in their child from infancy on. Without feelings of self-worth, no human being—infant, child or adult—can be truly happy. Whenever an infant is faced with a new and frightening situation, self-esteem may be enhanced or destroyed.

At a year of age, my friend's daughter reacted at being left at the day care center by screaming at the top of her lungs until her mother reappeared. Nothing the teachers did or said could comfort the child. My friend, fortunately, identified with her daughter's problem, recalling a time in her own childhood when she had felt abandoned and helpless. Therefore, she put off returning to work for awhile. By the time Jenny was three, she felt secure enough to wave happily whenever her mother left her at the day care center on the way to her part-time job.

If my friend had forced her daughter to stay at the day care center against her will, demanding that the child conform immediately to her adult wishes, or had slyly slipped away while her daughter's back was turned (a stratagem practiced by too many insensitive parents), Jenny might have acquired feelings of intense distrust, feelings which might endure for a lifetime.

In working with children who have found themselves in new, frightening situations, I have found this works: Allow ample time for confidence to grow; hold a child close, letting him push away when *he* feels ready to accept the challenge.

Whether a child comes out a winner or a loser in the game of self-confidence depends on the abundance or absence of love and understanding parents give. It is the wise parent who is there in time of crises to help, to listen and to love.

According to Dr. David Goodman, author of *A Parents' Guide to the Emotional Needs of Children,* adventuresomeness, fearlessness, and independence are the outcome of feeling absolutely secure in regard to parents. A child needs to know that his parents will be there. A youngster learns to feel safe in his universe by feeling secure at home.

When it comes to plain, old-fashioned courtesy, parents are prone to apply it liberally to casual acquaintances and visitors, yet are miserly when it comes to their own offspring. Children, we reason, are small and young so they don't warrant such niceties. Yet children are also intelligent, and they know when their dignity has been affronted.

I attended a meeting recently where a young mother sat directly in front of me with her one-year-old daughter. The baby was dressed in yellow with a matching ribbon taped to her wispy hair. *How good she is,* I thought, remembering the trying times I had experienced whenever I had tried to attend such adult functions with my young children.

Near the end of the discussion, the baby began to fuss. Instead of excusing herself and exiting early, the mother muffled the infant's crying with her gloved hand. If the mother had witnessed the expression of fear and rage on her small daughter's face, I am certain she would have refrained from that cruel gesture.

Through her crying the infant was attempting communication, telling her mother in the only way she knew, "See what a good sport I was. I sat through this whole thing for you. Now, I am tired, wet and hungry. Please—let's go home!"

Dr. Theodore Isaac Rubin, writing in *Compassion and Self-Hate,* tells about his seven-year-old son and his daughter, who was four. As they boarded the school bus one morning, his son told the driver, "Wait a minute. Another person is getting on." For days after that, the younger sister glowed with wonder, repeating over and over, "I am a *person!*"

As a very little girl, I relished shopping trips with my white-haired great-aunt, a lady with a whimsical, child-pleasing sense of humor. Invariably whenever we started home, her wicker basket laden with our purchases, she would turn and ask me, "Now which way do we go?" Proudly I would lead the way, directing her to that familiar street where she lived.

Whenever we value and respect a child's opinion and judgment we contribute enormously to his sense of self-worth. Recently when a neighbor's toddler commented on a "pink" cow, the little boy's father gently agreed that it was a pretty color. The father reasoned his son had many years to learn that some cows are brown and white, not pink.

Few families, if indeed any, ever achieve perfection in their inter-family relationships. Yet it is possible for parents to be tuned-in, to be aware of times of special need, times in a toddler's life when he may require special consideration.

For example, in one of the summer swim sessions which I teach at our community pool, I was coaching a little girl who violently resisted my attempts to teach her to float on her back. When I instructed her to wrap her arms around my neck, to "hang on tight," she did. At first I felt my neck was in a vise, then ever so gradually she relaxed her hold.

At last her breath came slowly and evenly. After several sessions, she felt secure enough to let go. Because she had felt in charge of the situation, she gradually gained the confidence she needed to push her crutch away.

Success fosters self-esteem—and nothing feels quite so good to a timid youngster! Even the most confident child, at one time or another, experiences an intense need to be held close. In times of trouble and turmoil, parents should honor a child's special needs.

Ideally, we must strive for a balance between protection and independence. Parents who are too protective foster dependence, just as those who push their children away create feelings of inadequacy.

According to child psychologists, parents must

allow a child a degree of independence to grow and develop according to his own inner calling. Whenever possible, let the youngster decide when he is ready for independence. Let the child break the bond, prove the mother-crutch is not necessary. It is the parent's responsibility to be "on standby," to offer warm encouragement and support whatever the child's decision. In this way a child learns to rely on his own inner resources, but with solid moral support.

Being a good parent is really a tall order, full of contradiction. Parenting calls for giving with no strings attached. We must be available to proffer our strength, while striving to become obsolete in our children's lives. We should be there "to hang on tight," to give generously of human warmth, love and security, so that someday we can give our nestling to the world, knowing that he will be strong and secure, sure enough of himself to look life's many adversaries straight in the eye.

When practiced on a day-to-day basis, compassion breeds compassion, respect begets respect. As parents we must constantly remind ourselves during the hectic blunder and bustle of bringing up children: *Never trounce on pint-sized dignity.*

10
LOVE:
Cloak Of The Fledgling

With his shock of unruly black hair and his deep brown-blue eyes, you are certain that never before in the history of the world was there another like your baby boy. And how right you are! At first, you regard him as extremely fragile, but soon you come to realize how tyrannical this seven pounds of dimpled flesh can be!

Unfortunately, unlike a new automobile, babies don't come with an owner's manual. Physical care and feeding are fairly routine, you find, but what about his spiritual needs? How do you go about teaching him right from wrong? You want only good things for him, *the very best.* Yet, is there danger that you will focus so much attention on him that he will grow up rebellious and disobedient?

Thousands of factors contribute to the development of a child's budding personality. The home, the community, the church, the school—all influence the child for good or for ill. Dr. William E. Homan, writing in his book, *Child Sense,* says that there are three needs that are basically essential to the development of a healthy, normal personality. First and foremost among these is *love*. Never can there be too much love in a youngster's life.

Recent research at Johns Hopkins University involving controlled studies of 26 mothers and infants established that it pays to pay attention to your infant. According to these scientific tests, it is impossible to spoil an infant by too much loving attention.

Scientific studies have further proven that mothers who catered to their child's blossoming individuality and potential had an easier time raising cooperative children. Follow-up studies of those infants at Johns Hopkins revealed that those babies who had had their needs met promptly were more cooperative and easier to handle than those whose mothers responded slowly to their cries.

Spoiling is the result of too many gifts and too few demands—too many carnival rides, too many teddy bears, and too many indulgences without "thank you" or "I love you" in return. Takers are made, not born, and too much too soon is as disabling to a child as too little too late! Spoiling is never the result, however, of too much personal attention and loving guidance.

As parents, we are always in danger of giving too much or too little discipline or independence or material goods. But in loving we can err only by not giving enough of ourselves and of our love. Love is bestowed as a free gift, no strings attached. With sufficient love, a child can withstand the most horrible buffetings of fate. The pressures of the world outside are little to the child whose inner world is secure.

"It's very easy to raise a psychotic child," my sister, a registered nurse, commented after a tour of duty in a psychiatric ward. "All you have to do is withhold love!"

Psychotics are emotional cripples. Such persons cannot give or receive love because they have never experienced it themselves. Crippling of this kind is far more painful than a physical handicap. Few controlled studies have been done to establish the effects of the total absence of love in human lives, yet in our mental wards, prisons and ghettos there is evidence galore which reveals the misery in human terms reaped by the absence of love.

Love is vital, but besides oodles of loving concern, a child requires *discipline.* Parents are in a quandary as to what discipline entails. When, how much, what kind? Should I spank? If I do, how hard and how long? Isn't there some ready-made formula I can adopt and employ to ease these tricky problems in discipline as they arise? What should I do, for instance, when my three year old astounds the community by shinnying up a flagpole during the Fourth of July parade? Or sets grandpa's haystack afire? Or substitutes sand for water in the family car's radiator?

In *How to Parent,* Dr. Fitzhugh Dodson gives some vital clues in solving the sticky issues of discipline. "Individualize discipline!" he contends. In other words, tailor your lessons for each child. Utilize the differences that occur naturally among children. The spanking that works wonders on one youngster might only intimidate another.

Self-esteem is enhanced when guidance is lovingly administered and geared to a child's special needs and personality. Punishment teaches children how not to behave, while discipline gives them an alternative to objectionable doings. Children tend to repeat undesirable behavior when they are not instructed regarding an alternative.

Dr. Dodson emphasizes that discipline is ideally a teaching device. We must employ discipline for the sake of the child, not the parent—never to relieve the pent-up frustrations and anger we often feel as adults.

Another valuable teaching aid is letting a child experience the natural consequences of his actions. In this way he learns discernment. If your son or daughter, for instance, neglects homework in favor of an evening of television, don't bail him out. Instead, let him reap the natural reward—even if it means a failing grade. Next time he will make a point of doing his homework before switching on the television set.

Make demands of your child! Let him know which things you approve or disapprove. Guide, teach, gear him to a world of realities, consequences, both pleasant and unpleasant. Exchange ideas! And during this process, utilize the opportunity to relay Christian principles, your heartfelt ideas about right and wrong.

Independence, the third essential ingredient to a well-integrated personality, is vital in aiding a youngster in establishing a toehold in this slippery world. Respect even the youngest child's urge for freedom. Let even a toddler try various things for himself. From babyhood on, encourage those accomplishments that lead to self-esteem.

Many activities bring with them the threat of self-destruction, and dangers should be pointed out and dealt with realistically. Still, little ones must have the right to try, to hurt themselves even, to fail—not once but over and over throughout life. For that is how we learn to do anything in this world.

The earliest stirrings of independence begin in the cradle with the lifting and turning of the neck and head, the refusal of the nipple when full, the waving of tiny arms and the kicking of dimpled legs, culminating at last in the turning over from back to stomach.

Between six and twelve months, baby will jerk the spoon from your hand and insist on feeding himself. It takes valiant restraint to ignore the mashed potatoes and gravy in his hair and eyes! Soon he will be demanding a place at the table and will become almost civilized in table manners. Seek to channel childish exuberance into positive outlets. Stifle not that dynamic quality that distinguishes the child from the sedate adult!

A Senate Subcommittee investigating juvenile delinquency discovered that the one common ingredient lacking in the lives of juvenile lawbreakers was caring, concerned parents. Even children from the wealthiest families, they discovered, failed to develop conscience when loving guidance was withheld. A child reasons, *nobody cares about me, so why should I care about anyone else?*

A special television program dealing with juvenile violence was aired recently. Society's flotsam and jetsam, products of overburdened, alcoholic, drug-addicted, impotent and uncaring parents, these kids were almost without conscience. Stealing and killing was a way of life for these youngsters. How did they get that way? What in their lives stifled the normal development of self-control?

Conrad Jensen, a police officer in New York City, says that parents of young lawbreakers fail their children by not giving them discipline. Like wild animals roaming the streets and alleys, these children had not been shown right from wrong. Juvenile crime, he said, is the outcome of lack of discipline.

Stunted conscience is also a by-product of spiritual neglect which occurs even in a setting of material plenty. Unless someone relays standards to a child, morality cannot be learned. Parents who do not do right themselves cannot hope to pass on to their children ideals about right and wrong.

That small voice that dictates what is good and what is evil does not spring up accidentally. Conscience is a product of parental caring, discipline and love. From infancy on, relaying Christian values becomes a parent's foremost concern.

One of the juveniles interviewed on the television special told how he would go into the streets smashing skulls, knifing, hurting and maiming others after being beaten by his father. A product of abuse, neglect and almost total rejection, this young man passed on to the world what he had learned from his parents.

Many parents inadvertently go about the business of discipline backwards: "If you want Mommy to love you, then you must first be good." Instead of, "I love you absolutely. And I will always love you, no matter what happens."

This is the kind of love that Christ extends to members of the human race when we accept Him as our personal Saviour. This is the love that allows for even grievous mistakes, with rectification through confession and forgiveness.

Conditional love, however ("I'll love you if . . ."), breeds low self-esteem. When used as a tool of discipline, conditional love destroys self-worth. Held like a hickory stick over an insecure child, love proffered and then withdrawn becomes a form of cruelty. Those who employ conditional love as discipline seem to have a neurotic need to bully others. Insecurity marks the child who must constantly battle to win parental support.

Remember: As parents, our goal in disciplining a child is to establish self-esteem for himself and Christian concern for others. If we want our children to respect the rights and feelings of others, we must begin by respecting the rights and feelings of our children. Loving guidance teaches. Loving guidance ultimately conveys inner discipline. It bestows ideals and concepts about right and wrong, good and evil.

Love works miracles! Loved for himself, a child feels valued as an individual. Christ-centered love can overcome seemingly hopeless situations.

Vow today that you will not cause your child to go astray through indifference or rejection. Love your child. Discipline him because you love him. In so doing, you will be gradually guiding him to the healthy independence he'll need as an adult.

Vow never to put things before your relationship with this most precious human being. Save time each day to relay your love and your concern for each child in your care. Be available, always on call, even while on the job. Make arrangements so that your child can discuss those things that trouble and perplex him during the growing up years.

Determine not to be a "backstage mother," pushing him into a style of life or occupation that satisfies your own frustrated ego. For God has given you an etching, not a print, a voice rather than an echo. Vow to help your precious charges grow every day in self-esteem.

All of God's children are special, and it is our duty as parents to relay this message to those little ones in our charge. Obedience and conscience are the natural by-products of loving guidance. When a child feels esteemed, when his individuality is honored, it follows as night after day that he will return the gift in the form of cooperative, loving Christian behavior!

11
ANGER:
The Fledgling's First Chirp

One of the blessings of full-time nestkeeping is the close involvement we can experience with our children's blossoming emotions. As a child advances in maturity there are conflicts—differences of opinion among peers and family members. Frequently such frustrations result in temperamental outbursts of varying degrees.

Temper uncontrolled can be a dangerous thing and a serious personality flaw. A mother's task, because of her close association with the child, is to help the child control, understand and accept the temperament that God has bestowed.

If your son or daughter is too timid to stand up for himself, or is always flying off the handle, perhaps he has not learned to use anger appropriately. As we get older we learn (hopefully) to tolerate more and more frustration without getting angry. As adults we have much experience in coping with and defusing our angry feelings. As a result, we sometimes tend to be unsympathetic to Junior's temperamental outbursts. By our attitude we let those in our charge know that when it comes to anger we expect nothing short of adult control.

Using anger in an appropriate manner, like any other skill, is learned by children over a period of years through experience. The pain of growing up can be greatly lessened by understanding adults who realize the uses and purposes of this God-given emotion.

Often Christian parents set unrealistic standards for their children, asking them to always stifle this negative emotion, no matter how severely provoked. But according to a host of psychologists, a child's anger should not always be suppressed.

When little Jim Simpson bloodied Oliver Sanders' nose during a sandpile altercation, Jim's parents were dismayed by their son's lack of civility. No matter that their son had been teased and taunted, that Oliver had repeatedly thrown sand in his playmate's eyes, captured his favorite toy truck, and knocked down his sand castle. No matter that Jim had attempted to resolve the conflict in a peaceful manner, warning over and over, "Don't do that, Ollie!"

Oliver persisted in his onslaught against his playmate, seeing just how far he could go. Jim had the feeling there was only one sensible recourse, physical action.

Still, Jim's parents could not accept their son's display of temper, especially not in a physical sense. They practiced the Golden Rule in their dealings; why couldn't little Jim?

They lectured their son on the evils of losing one's

temper, on playground etiquette, on the right and wrong ways of behaving, which certainly did not include striking back.

Stoicly little Jim refused to become playland's Caspar Milquetoast in order to please his parents. Sagely he continued to defend himself whenever circumstances required. Consequently he came to be respected, even liked, by the neighborhood boys. They knew that Jim never instigated a fight, yet he was quick to respond to aggression on the part of bullies.

According to the latest mental health findings, Jim's instincts had served him well. His inner senses had told him that anger does have its purpose, that his child's dignity had to be maintained.

Why were the Simpsons so intent on stripping their son of all defenses in a world of sand in the eyes, fists and teeth? They were not evidently aware that anger is a God-given emotion. They failed to realize that self-defense is a right of every American—even Christians!

Had Jim conformed to his parents' wishes, becoming a saint in miniature to please his mother and father, he would surely have become a patsy for the neighborhood ruffians. Did God want Jim to take Oliver's repeated punishment, his constant harrassment, his taunting remarks of "Fraidy Cat! Fraidy Cat!"?

I don't think so. God does not want His children to become wilted violets, suppressing every negative emotion. He would not have Jim channel his anger underground into his subconscious, to vent it later in teasing, tattling and sarcasm against his older brother and younger sister. He would not want Jim to hoard his hostilities against Oliver, using his pent-up emotions in cruelty to animals—kicking the family dog, pulling the cat's tail. Or, as is sometimes the case, He would not want Jim to become overly good and timid, steering clear of involvement with his peers so that his secret hostilities could not leak out.

In spite of a messy bloody nose, Jim had handled his emotion in an appropriate manner. His action had served a dual purpose. Jim had rid himself of frustration as well as demonstrated clearly to the neighborhood toughs, "Don't mess around with Jim."

Dr. James Dobson believes that a child ought to be allowed to strike back. According to Dobson in his book *Dare to Discipline,* when youngsters play together they establish which toy truck, swing, trike, or bicycle is most desirable. Frequently a member of the group discovers he can control the playground by plying force, aiming a fist, or trouncing on those who are too timid to put up a fuss.

Passive resistance, according to Dobson, might be intelligent strategy for monks in isolated temples, but parents who insist that a child never fight back are conditioning their offspring for an unreal world, a world chock full of ruffians who have never even heard of the Golden Rule.

Feelings of anger are normal, according to Dr. Theodore Isaac Rubin, former president of the American Institute of Psychoanalysis and author of *The Angry Book.* "All human beings get angry, and

I am certain the saints did too," he wrote. "Feeling angry is universal among the human species. It is as basic as feeling hungry, lonely, loving, or tired. The ability to feel angry and to respond in some way to that feeling is in us from birth. Have you ever seen a newborn baby cry and scream, and get red with rage?"

Until he learns more appropriate responses to anger, the preschooler will often express his negative feelings by biting, hitting, shoving and screaming. If riled enough, he might resort to tantrums—lying on his back, kicking and screaming, flailing arms and legs.

When anger strikes, even the smallest human is transformed into a different being, physically and psychologically. The human body chemistry is entirely rearranged by this powerful emotion. The various glands and organs of the body instigate major physiological changes. The heart races. Blood centered in the liver and stomach is diverted into the large muscles. Sugar from the liver is poured into the bloodstream. Adrenalin floods the system and breathing becomes charged.

Anger is a physical entity, something very real that must be dealt with, talked out, prayed about, released. If it is not, and instead is blocked or stored, it will accumulate in the human subconscious, resulting in maladies or self-destructive mechanisms such as head-banging, sleep-walking, nightmares, hyperactivity, hypertension, nail biting, teeth grinding, headaches, self-mutilation. In many cases, unresolved rage manifests itself in acts of violence toward others.

Psychologists tell us that when children are afraid to express anger they sometimes employ substitute targets for the release of their less-than-positive feelings. "My children are angels at home. My husband and I do not tolerate misbehavior," one mother boasted. Yet at teacher conferences she discovered that her youngsters were generally disruptive in the classroom.

Or consider the case of little Andy, who harbors feelings of rage against an older brother who teases and mercilessly torments him. Because Andy fears his bigger brother, he takes out his negative feelings on smaller boys in the neighborhood.

Wise parents adopt a sympathetic attitude toward a child's feelings of anger. One father I know tells his toddler during temperamental outbursts, "I know why you're so mad. I would be, too." For most children such a reaction is very soothing. Just knowing that somebody understands and sympathizes with our feelings has a mollifying effect on us and it serves also as a door opener for parents to wider communication in the future.

Sometimes a child's anger masks earlier frustration. We as parents must learn to decode a child's angry responses. In her book, *Your Child's Self-Esteem,* Dorothy Briggs explains, "Knowing that anger covers a prior emotion helps you deal with it more reasonably, both in yourself and in your children."

Three year old Kenneth lashed out at his mother when she refused him another turn down the slide.

"I hate you," he bellowed. Instead of adding her anger to his, which was her first impulse, she realized that he was merely reacting to an afternoon of accumulated frustration. Hadn't he spent over two hours waiting for her while she chose a dress pattern and material?

Instead of punishing him for his outburst, she apologized. In turn he told her, "I am sorry, Mama. I really do love you."

We have been conditioned to think that feeling angry and showing it is "bad"—not normal, even inhuman. "He can't control his temper," we say gravely, shaking our heads. More accurately, we mean that he has not grown up enough to use anger in a skillful and appropriate manner, to defuse it before it explodes and uses him.

It is our duty as parents to help our children become philosophical in dealing with life's many frustrations and disappointments. We must emphasize that Christians do not hit or hurt or lash out at others, even when hurt. As Christian parents, we should teach our children the futility of fighting; yet, we must not force a youngster to stand passively by while being clobbered by cold-blooded peers.

It is good mental health never to let the sun go down on our wrath, therefore we should attempt to create the kind of home where anger is talked out, prayed about, where there are no longstanding grudges, no cesspools of hate. We must work to establish the kind of atmosphere where people are able to forgive and forget quickly.

Using anger instead of letting anger use us involves a decision-making process—when to turn the other cheek or when to take a stand. In His ministry, Christ used anger to overcome the money-changers in the temple; yet He also often turned the other cheek and went the extra mile for others.

We need to strive to teach our children constructive decision-making processes, so they too will reflect a Christlike image.

12
TIMING:
To Push Or Protect?

Conscientious nestkeeping calls for special insight.

Mothers often need a deep spiritual perception in dealing with sensitive children. Too busy, many women skim over special needs while regimenting, scolding, riding roughshod over tender hurts.

Thoughtlessly, we can cause untold damage to tender psyches! Too early separations are one area we must be extremely careful of, for children can be indelibly marked by emotional suffering that can occur when pushed out of the nest too abruptly.

When my youngest, for example, was two years old I was asked to teach at a Bible camp for two weeks. "We'll have a sitter in town," our minister said. "You can leave Kirsten with her."

The camp was fourteen miles out of town at a beautiful lake. I was eager to communicate Christ to these young people. However, leaving Kirsten every day at a sitter's was impossible. I had left her only occasionally, never for more than an hour at a time. And when I had, she had always cried as if her heart was broken. I couldn't bear to leave her, not even for this wonderful Christian experience.

"I am sorry," I said. "I will come only if it is all right to bring Kirsten along too."

I sensed that our young minister did not approve, although he did not say so until later. I was able to go, and took my youngest along. She played happily with her toys while I taught my class. The rest of the day we were together.

The day before the Bible camp ended, the staff sat around talking. There was another teacher whose boy was the same age as Kirsten, and she had left him in town with the sitter.

"Jamie," she complained, "screams every morning when I leave him. But it's good for him. He's got to learn to do without me."

Everyone agreed, some saying you never know when you might have to go to the hospital and that it is good to get them "broke" early. The minister also agreed and gave a lengthy lecture on the dangers of over-protective mothering.

I felt the sting of their words, yet somehow I knew in my heart that in my case, I was right.

The following winter when Kirsten was two and a half, I tried several times to leave her in her Sunday School class. She would cry and cling to my skirts. I didn't make her stay, though the teachers agreed that I should. I felt she was not ready for such a grown-up experience.

Then one Sunday she surprised us! Clutching her little Bible and coin holder, she marched toward her class when we entered the church. I started to follow, but decided to let her go alone.

It was a grown-up little lady who went down that church corridor, and later the teacher told me her behavior had been perfect.

My instinct had been right for this two year old. Some children must not be "broke"; rather, they must break away by themselves. The test for parents is knowing when to protect and when to push a little!

13
LEARNING TO LOVE:
God's Special Houseguests

One of the goals of Christian parents should be to instill in youngsters the quality of concern for other living beings. What better way than through the responsibility of a pet?

Recently on "Good Morning, America," a couple appeared with their baby and two cats. The cats had been awarded a medal for heroism, for when fire broke out in the family's home, the pets had awakened the sleeping mother-to-be, thus saving the lives of both mother and unborn child.

Although my encounters with the feline species have been less heroic, I still feel a warm kinship with these furry creatures. Webster defines a cat as a carnivorous mammal, long domesticated and kept by man as a pet for catching rats and mice. Not so! Webster is wrong. Everyone knows that cats are brought home by boys and girls to be petted and pampered and fed a nutritionally complete cat food from a box or a can. Most of the cats I know wouldn't recognize a mouse if it was dangled in front of their nose.

OCCUPATION: NESTBUILDER

What's a parent to do when the children appear with a purring, kneading, sweater-snagging ball of fluff? How do you ignore pleading eyes as they deliver a Madison Avenue speech on the joys of cat ownership? When they inform you that the lady across the street has a mother cat who recently deposited a litter of ten in the neighbor's husband's machine shop, do you think of torn draperies, shredded furniture, expensive trips to the vet, those ubiquitous clumps of hair that float through the air—not to mention the ringworm and subsequent doctor bills?

This one, a short-haired panther, with soft cornflower-blue eyes, appears innocent. How could he possibly cause any trouble? I weaken as they inform me with teary eyes that the lady has been warned sternly by the man of her house, "Get rid of them or else!"

The "or else" brings tears to *my* eyes.

"Can we, Mama?"

"May we?"

"All right."

That night we discover that, although innocent-looking, our new feline is insomnious. A steady caterwaul emerges from the garage so we move its bed onto the front porch. That concession, however, fails to stop the noise, but only makes it more audible.

"How can anything so small make so much noise?" my husband growls, covering his ears with his pillow.

"Maybe he was weaned too soon!" I murmur.

Henry proved to be a Henrietta, and in due time we were presented with a bountiful litter. Taking to the streets, the kids themselves became vendors of kittens.

Sharing your domicile with a cat has drawbacks, yet there are some blessings. Cats do not require a lot of attention, and in a household where everyone clamors for a busy mother's time, this is an asset.

Given a box of sand, a kitten will use it instinctively. Turned outside, they are meticulous about digging a hole and carefully covering it with dirt. Transparent tips of a cat's claws can be trimmed, thus eliminating scratches and shredded furniture. Toms who are neutered do not urinate on the walls and stay close to home, rather than indulging in a sordid nightlife.

As I look back over my childhood, I think how bleak it might have been without my cat, Junior. Early one winter morning I found him huddled under the steps, a pitiful clump of ice. A neighbor's dog had rolled him into a shivering ball of ice and snow. We rushed him inside, placing him beside our furnace. My father looked him over, pronouncing his benediction. Stubbornly my sister and I refused to give him up. All night we kept a prayer going for our little animal, and in the morning, the bedraggled kitten hungrily lapped up the milk we gave him.

Junior eventually grew into a lion of a cat. Whenever we dressed him up in doll clothes, he couldn't have been more indignant. Up and down the sidewalk we bumped him in my doll carriage, with his bonneted ears perched gruffly on the back of his head. Yet never did he bite or scratch.

Junior reveled in teasing my pop. He would skitter by his chair, his long tail flashing, challenging my father to give his waving tail an ever so gentle tug. Junior could be fierce too, and the dogs in our neighborhood gave our yard a wide berth.

Even in my adult life as wife and mother, various four-legged friends have come to us in strange ways over the years. We have hosted cats, dogs, gerbils, hamsters, and turtles (in addition to parakeets and goldfish). But certain pets have marked our lives indelibly, like the little pup that stayed only a few short weeks but won our hearts completely.

I haven't thought about our Bonnie Lassie in a long time. Today I wouldn't have thought of her either, except for that shell of a might-have-been doghouse pushed back underneath the basement steps. It had been a project undertaken by my son for our small pup. A clumsy job, yet each nail had been his solemn declaration of love, driven by inept, childish hands.

It seems ages ago. I remember waiting there by the schoolhouse door for my husband to finish his Cub Scout meeting. There by the entrance, the local Lutheran minister positioned himself. Quietly he and his young son set up their business, and I smiled when he soon appeared with a large cardboard box overflowing with puppies. His youngster tacked up a crudely-lettered bit of advertising: "The Only Real Free Love In the World, Puppy Love!"

Then the man of the cloth attempted to make puppy ownership as vital as salvation to those who passed by.

"Now really, we don't need a puppy," I said, protesting over his appeal to my sense of Christian charity. Prospective puppy owners brisked by him without a nod, while kids tugged relentlessly at coat sleeves and hems of their parents.

When I inquired about their breed, the minister informed me that the mother was dubiously beagle, and the father a neighborhood mongrel, mostly German Police. One of the pups however, had been fathered by a silver beagle—registered and with pedigree. A high school girl that very minute was bargaining with her parents for its ownership. When she appeared cheerlessly with the tiny animal cradled in her arms, I gazed into that puppy's eyes and a shock of recognition passed between us.

The teenager exchanged a sorrowful glance with the pastor and placed the pup back in the box. It rejoined its brothers and sisters with glee. The entire litter welcomed her back with sloshy licks as they fell upon her. All of them doubled her in size.

Taking a dog at this stage would be insane! There was a dangerous highway fifty feet from our front door. It bustled day and night with trucks, buses and speeding cars. Dog ownership was out of the question. We could not risk a puppy's life, I told the minister. Added to that, I was in the process of toilet training our two-year-old and adding a pup as a trainee would be crazy. Further, my husband disliked dogs, city ones at least.

Still, she seemed so special. The way she had of cocking her head to one side with a decided air of aristocracy was winning me. I harbored the undemocratic notion that her brothers and sisters were bound to grow up as real dredges on society. To me, those mongrels seemed fair game for the city dogcatcher. Yet their dainty little sister had won my heart.

"I'll take her," I said, mesmerized by her sleek and pendulous ears. In her eyes was definite intelligence, obviously lacking in her siblings. Now I feared that the clergyman might sense my eagerness and attach a price to this lady of obvious distinction. Or the teenager, I reasoned, was bound to return after making another plea to her parents. So I snatched the pup and ran!

Rustic autumn had settled over our small community. Nights had turned brisk. Beneath my hurried feet leaves crackled. The pup huddled inside my jacket as my two-year-old hustled behind us to keep up.

At home, I nervously hunted a box amid basement clutter. A nice-sized apple carton would do, and I lined it with rags. Upstairs my older daughter was preparing for bed. Amid squeals of delight, she said, "But what about Dad?"

"Sh, here he comes!"

The door slammed shut as my husband entered —the man who only tolerated useful dogs, seeing-eye ones, or those they had employed on his Montana ranch as herders of sheep and cows. "Isn't she precious?" my daughter whispered. In one of those wonderful moments of shared delight, our hands met as we reached to stroke her silky back.

Later before going to bed, my husband made his nightly check upstairs. A whimper beneath the covers of my daughter's bed aroused his curiosity. His investigation brought forth our puppy, callously hoisted by the nape of its neck! Outside into the frost-embittered night he sent her. "You can find another home in the morning!" he said.

By morning, however, my husband had forgotten his stern command. So the four of us—myself, John, Jackie and Kirsten—got our heads together to conspire on a name for our newcomer. "Let's call her Lassie," my son suggested. "She's too pretty," my daughter said. I suggested Bonnie Lassie. And so it was.

Through her canine sense of intuition our little dog seemed to sense a war of wills going on over her presence in our household. Courageously she undertook the mission to win over the head of our house. With one ear off balance she courted him. She seemed to sense his moods. At first she served as foot warmer. Later, she graduated into his lap. Ultimately she won his favor as an almost constant companion.

Our two-year-old and the beagle became inseparable as a team. Next-door neighbors still chuckle about the crisp morning they glanced out their window to see our beagle pup and flashes of our little one's bare baby bottom as they frisked together in the backyard.

My son, then almost eleven, designed a doghouse. Wondering what he was doing after school I followed him into the basement. With hammer and saw he undertook his labor of love, constructing a wobbly puppy shelter.

A persistent drizzle of rain splashed on the highway one Friday morning as I pulled open the curtains. Our little dog slept in her usual haunt beside my husband's recliner. That noon she greeted as usual the children as they came in from school for their lunches. Then she perched by the door, one ear erect and oscillating, awaiting the whir of my husband's tires in the driveway.

Friday was our day to shop. That afternoon when we went to the grocery store, we left the dog behind in the care of our two older children.

When we returned, a gang of frightened kids met us. *Something is the matter,* I thought. When we got out of the car, our oldest led us to the front porch. He lifted a towel ever so carefully from a box where the dead puppy lay. In mournful tones our children told us that they had gone across the street to play, forgetting ever so briefly the little dog who tagged faithfully at their heels. The speeding car that had broken her tiny neck had probably not even been jolted.

"If only," we began. But it was too late. All the "if onlies" in the world could not bring our Bonnie Lassie back.

Burial fell to the man of our house. He went stoically for his shovel. As he placed the small box in the back of his rig, he checked a tear with the cuff of his plaid coat.

14
READING:
The Fledgling Tries His Wings

Considerate parenting pays off.

Respect begets respect. Now that my older two are teenagers, the benefits of earlier dutiful parenting are flowing back to us. This does not mean that my children are perfect, but they are wonderfully considerate. We have a happy rapport that I sense is missing in homes where sensitivity to children's special needs is rarely displayed.

Generally my children delight me with their humor and good will. Rather than going through the trials of adolescent misbehaviour and rebellion, our relationship grows fonder with each passing year. We share many joys and interests. One of the delights we enjoy together is reading.

When my thirteen year old daughter finished Louisa May Alcott's *Little Women* she turned to me with flashing green eyes and exclaimed, "That's the best book I have ever read!"

I remembered having that same feeling after

reading it as a girl about her age. Jo, Beth, Meg and Amy were real, alive girls. Reading it again as an adult filled me with the same tingling sense of wonder. I felt somehow renewed, overwhelmed by the emotion that life is chock-full with meaning, purpose, and love—in spite of daily headlines proclaiming the opposite.

My children have established the habit of reading, and I am extremely thankful. A taste for the written word can be a Godsend on a rainy or snowbound day, on those long summer and Christmas vacations. What could possibly take the place of cozy winter afternoons by the fire? Or lazy summer days in the hammock with lemonade and a good book? Truly, I feel fortunate that my children's lives are filled with good literature.

Reading, as I see it, enhances their living by enlarging their scope. Their ability to comprehend an increasingly secular world is made easier through their almost daily encounter with the written word, enabling them to sort out right from wrong more easily. Still, I do not think that books have become a substitute for real life. My children ski, play tennis, basketball and baseball, babysit, deliver papers, participate in church and community activities.

Mom's bias acknowledged, my children seem to be different from the majority of their peers. I think it's because they read. I feel that they are somehow easier to get along with, to talk to, to reason with. They seem unusually understanding and compassionate toward fellow human beings and animals.

As I said, we're all far from perfect, yet we have

learned to disagree (at least most of the time) agreeably. It is very satisfying for me to watch them grow spiritually and emotionally as they absorb new truth through their Bible stories and Christian magazines. As they are exposed to a broad perspective of wholesome literature, they seem far more able to cope with the various problems that come up in their young lives.

Parents I have talked with agree that bringing kids up morally straight is made easier when children love to read. Reading is the most valuable hobby a child can have. Some parents complain, "My kids read nothing but the funnies." To my way of thinking, and as even some experts contend, this is not entirely bad. At least they are reading. Comics do offer a beginning by exposing youngsters to others like themselves who try, fail, and sometimes triumph. Comics also provide a spark of interest that can be kindled and sometimes ignited into a lively interest in the printed word by concerned adults.

Most readers are made, not born. The love of reading has to be cultivated in almost any child. The sooner we establish the habit of reading and foster the love of words in our offspring, the better. Starting in infancy, if we read aloud simple nursery rhymes and prayers, helping tiny fingers as they turn the pages, we are nurturing a child's budding interest in the English language.

At barely six months my oldest delighted in being held as I pointed out pictures in *Better Homes & Gardens,* the daily newspaper, and Sears & Roebuck. As he grasped for the pictured object, invariably his eager fingers would crumple the pages. So what! Those pages were destined for the compost heap anyway.

After the birth of my second child, the unrelenting routine of infant care was brightened for me by reading to her from popular women's magazines. I got some fun reading done that way, and since my singing voice is not of lullaby quality, my reading to her provided the cradle songs that she would have missed otherwise. By the time this little girl was three she would tell me, "Sit down, I will read you a story." I had read to her so much that she knew her simple stories by heart.

Shared reading provides shining moments to be savored for years to come, opportunities for snuggling close—the physical intimacy deemed so essential by anthropologists, psychologists, and psychiatrists for a secure and truly happy childhood.

A teacher friend tells me that she can easily detect those children whose parents have invested much time reading to them at home. Listening skills, vocabulary, social intelligence, and attention span are all aided by an early encounter with the written word.

Reading repetition sharpens a child's listening skills and improves visual perception. For children who have not been exposed to the singsong world of Mother Goose, acquiring the skill of reading can prove difficult. Conscientious parents and grandparents will therefore not send their little ones off to school with a handicap; read and reread those little prayers, stories and rhymes, no matter how tiresome!

A teacher friend was concerned about a pupil who was failing. He simply could not grasp the basic fundamentals of reading, so she called in the youngster's mother, hoping to find an ally.

"Read to him," she encouraged.

"I have," the parent exclaimed defensively. "His father gave him a book for his birthday once and I read it to him."

This mother, like many others, did not understand that reading readiness requires more than skimming a book once or twice. According to various teachers I have talked to, it takes constant exposure to the same books on a regular basis to promote that degree of visual and verbal awareness essential to the first-grader's success with the written word.

For numerous children, magic doorways may be opened through good reading. Starting as toddlers with *Mother Goose* and simple Bible stories, a child advances in awareness. He learns that "might does not make right" through "David and Goliath," or that beauty can be only a matter of waiting to grow up, as depicted in "The Ugly Duckling," or through the adventures of "Snow White," that one should not indiscriminately accept the handouts of strangers.

Sometimes, too, these stories lighten a young mother's work day by getting her off her feet for awhile, while providing her children with positive moral examples to be more cheerful, mannerly and persistent.

In her *Bequest of Wings*, Annis Duff claims that

children who master the art of reading and who truly enjoy the written word are really lucky in that they acquire a sense of self-mastery and power in their lives. Independent reading provides personal satisfaction on an intense level. In Christian homes where children learn to love to read from an early age, many have an opportunity to begin independent Bible study at the age they are likely to benefit the most.

Certain children seem to be predestined bookworms. Others find enjoyment mainly in occupations that involve primarily physical activity. Yet many children can be enticed to read if they are tactfully motivated by their concerned parents. Sustaining an interest in the written word is no small accomplishment, especially in today's world with the twin distractions of television and radio. But it is not entirely impossible for parents to foster the love of reading in their children.

Start by letting your child observe your pleasure in the written word. Let him find you studying your Bible, reading the paper, perusing Christian magazines. Let him get acquainted with your public library; make trips to your church library a part of your schedule, too.

Purchase books for your child as gifts on birthdays and Christmas. Subscribe to a journal that is slanted toward the Christian youngster. Then, be available for the lively discussions that will ensue as a result of new ideas. Provide easily accessible space for books, a shelf or small bookcase. In your own reading, share those ideas and passages that inspire and move you. In turn, I have found, a child will come to you with stars in his eyes, saying, "Mom, listen to this!"

A friend of mine, the mother of four, works away from home full time in order to provide for her family. Still she finds the means to instill the love of good literature in her youngsters. Although she has little time for the leisurely pursuit of reading, she encourages her kids to read aloud to her while she irons.

In their home, space and time are set aside for reading. Many evenings her children are snug in their beds early so that they can spend an hour with a good book. For this family, bedside reading tables and lamps (built by a loving grandfather) provide an important part of their environment.

I will never forget the fertile reading ground of my grandmother's parlor. There I learned to truly treasure the written word. Bookcases lined with sturdy volumes stretched to the ceiling. On her shelves I discovered *Pilgrim's Progress,* Dickens, Emerson, Poe. Countless hours were spent there happily poring over her collection, as I found comfort and respite from the tensions of my day-to-day existence.

I have come to realize that not everything a child reads needs to be religious as long as it is wholesome and relevant to his world. When I made the mistake of insisting my child read exclusively "morally uplifting" books, he responded by quitting reading altogether. Only after I let up on my crusade did he begin to read again. Our impasse has culminated in a compromise: now he eagerly reads a magazine that emphasizes Christian principles along with his favorite subject. His teacher tells me, "He has read every book in our library on sports."

My son recently told me he found inspiration through reading to defeat an opponent with a 30-pound edge during a wrestling match. Through the understanding of Biblical truth he is learning to accept with equal grace both victory and defeat.

The "right to read"—even the ability to read—can be worthless unless we also learn to savor and enjoy the written word. One teacher described a "virtual miracle" when a non-reading youngster suddenly mastered the art of reading after discovering a subject that really fascinated him.

Truly, there is joy in reading! Your child can experience wholesome delight between the covers of a book. He can discover the Bible on his own, and discover for himself in a special way the person of Jesus Christ.

Envy the parents of children who love to read! Children who read are not often bored for, as my oldest put it, "There's just not time enough to read all the good books that have been written."

Other parents dash hither and yon in attempts to keep their offspring occupied. Constantly they invest in expensive games and gadgetry in order to satisfy their sons' and daughters' craving for excitement. But as connoisseurs of the written word many discover entire worlds of adventure, knowledge and guidelines for their young lives—without stirring from the rocking chair!

15
FEATHERING:
Wanting Is Worth Waiting

Possibly shortage of cold hard cash is one of the most annoying realities faced in my job as full-time wife and mother. My husband's single paycheck is often stretched and pinched. When it comes to feathering our nest, it seems there is never quite enough to cover today's inflationary prices, taxes, and things we want.

It is a great temptation for me in my impatience to depend on credit cards, to go ahead and purchase the things I think we must have before the dollars are in hand. Such a practice, however, can spell financial bankruptcy. Charging, as we all well know, merely puts off the payment date. And when all those bills start rolling in it is easy to become convinced that wanting is worth waiting after all!

The learned art of waiting serves me in the many annoyances and frustrations of being a nestbuilder. Patience is made, not born (babies are notoriously impatient!).

How slowly we learn to wait! A child waits for Christmas; a gardener waits for spring and warm earth; I wait in line at the supermarket—sometimes the most trying wait of all!

It's hard for me to wait for my husband when he comes home late from work, but I have learned to do it cheerfully, at least most of the time. It's hard to save the money and wait for a new carpet, but I am doing it. Waiting isn't easy; it is a learned art! I remember waiting to be sixteen; waiting for my husband to ask me to marry him; waiting for the wedding; waiting for my first baby, later for the second and six years after that my third; waiting for the loan to buy our first home.

Mother was right. Those things I wanted were all worth the waiting. When I read about people bombing buildings to right a wrong, impatient with their world, their vulnerable young faces concern me. I wish they had learned what my mother taught me: Just because you want something doesn't make it right for you to do wrong. If you wait you'll be glad; you may change your mind about things.

Again and again I have thanked God for my mother's guidance in my life, for I have at times been indignant about war, wasted tax money, pollution, chemicals added to my food, and dishonesty in high places.

Would my teenagers be among the bombers, the disillusioned, if I had not taught them, as my mother taught me: *Wanting is worth waiting?*

16
AT LAST:
Sweeping Out The Nest

Working mothers, overbusy in their own jobs, often neglect their children's right to feel accomplishment by doing simple tasks. Sometimes a hurried schedule makes it far easier to "do it myself" than to instruct unskilled youngsters in how to perform simple chores. Well-meaning moms and dads are tempted to pitch in because we don't like the messes created by inexpert fingers. Or we can't stand an amateur performance. Yet if we don't extend to children the right of trial-and-error, how will they ever learn to do anything well?

Doing for a child that which he can do for himself is a grave error, for work is essential to a balanced life. Kids who are not taught the dignity of work are deprived. Therefore helping your child overcome childish resistance to work becomes one of the prime concerns of the nestkeeper.

Children are naturally disinclined to work. A toddler can bound about from here to there, build a superstructure out of blocks, knock it down and start all over again. A youngster can bounce from one project to another without ever tiring. But ask this same energetic child to pick up his toys after play is over and more likely than not he will rebel, "I am too tired!" When the parent presses the point, the child might whine, cry or conduct a miniature sit-down strike.

To adult minds this doesn't make sense. Is the youngster just being contrary? How could just a few motions wear out a youngster who has exerted himself so eagerly all morning? If you can, think back to your own childhood. Try to recall your own childish disinclination to toil.

I remember when I was so lazy that walking across the room to hang up my coat was a major undertaking. I recall when I thought that doing one simple task in a day's time was a tremendous burden. Slowly, with my parents' understanding guidance, I overcame my natural sloth.

With the help and encouragement of my parents, I grew in responsibility. Gradually I took on more and more in terms of real labor. The summer I was twelve, I was baby-sitting for half a day. When I was fourteen, I taught swim lessons. By sixteen, I worked a full eight-hour day as a lifeguard at our local pool.

As Christian parents, we want our children to feel joy and pride in a job well done. In the Christian tradition, work and service to others is an essential ingredient to a well-ordered personality. We want our youngsters to come to know the pride of real accomplishment. We hope that someday they will realize a difficult task through to its completion and feel joy and pride of seeing a really worthwhile project through to its end. I want no loafers or welfare recipients in my house.

But how does a parent overcome a child's strong aversion to labor? And at what age should I expect my offspring to join the workaday world? For very young children—toddlers and preschoolers—the majority of the day is spent in free play. During this time growth is taking place. During make-believe a child grows by pretending what it is like to be an adult. For a period a child might become a teacher, a doctor, a mother, a farmer, or a truck driver. In this manner he or she "tries on" different lifestyles to see how they feel and fit. On a preschool level, career conditioning takes place in this way.

When a child enters school, free time becomes structured. In kindergarten he or she must channel childish spurts of energy into coloring a picture, fingerpainting, learning to print. By first grade, several hours a day are programmed for learning to read, write or spell. Addition and subtraction must be mastered, a major undertaking for young minds.

Still later, even more time is taken up by formal activities. Children learn skills that will lead them eventually into adult occupations. Duty and responsibility gradually replace childish activities at home and school. We expect increasingly more of the growing youngster. We expect that he or she keep his bed made and room tidy.

I remember teaching my seven-year-old son to sweep the kitchen floor. Oh, the moanings and groanings that accompanied this task! In his inexperience, he pushed dirt from one side of the floor to the other, all the while complaining loudly! Finally he caught on to sweeping all the dirt and scraps together in one big pile, then pushing them into the dustpan.

It is a mistake for parents to think that jobs even as basic as sweeping are instinctive to small children. Even the most basic tasks need to be demonstrated and explained, sometimes over and over. Sweeping a floor represents a major challenge to an inexperienced child. Be patient. Don't expect too much too soon from your youngster. It takes time for children to adjust to and cope with new tasks.

How can we teach them self-discipline? How can we show them that work can actually be fun? That all work is not drudgery? How do we instill the feeling of dignity in all work—that any job, no matter how menial, affords its doer a slice of human dignity? How do we convey that work is the way to independence? How do we tell them that those who do not work are dependent on those who do, that when we refuse to work we become society's luggage, to be carried by others?

We relay through our *own* work the pride we feel in a job completed. We can in this way pass on the reality that the deepest of life's satisfactions come through toil and hard work.

Only gradually should we attempt to increase a child's sense of responsibility. As toddlers, I asked my children to help me to do small tasks—tying shoes, buttoning clothes, picking up toys. In a few years I came to expect more. I assigned simple chores, emphasizing, "Mommy needs your help!"

Eventually their sense of fair play expanded. Willingly they took on projects by themselves. My older daughter, Jacque, for example, began to babysit for a friend when she was only nine. Ordinarily this would be too much responsibility for a girl so young. The friend, however, lived directly across the street, and my daughter knew that if she had any trouble she could call on me. I would be immediately available to help her out. Today, in her teens, she is much in demand as a reliable sitter, with mothers constantly calling for her services.

This summer my fifteen-year-old son, John, is working, mowing lawns. He was at first extremely reluctant, embarrassed by the fact that I had put his name and telephone number out over the radio proclaiming, "Dependable boy wants lawn jobs." But, at the root of his fear and embarrassment was the question, *Can I measure up? Can I please my customers?*

Most of us are naturally frightened by new experiences, some of us more than others. Many of us are concerned about our performance, what others might think of us. Can we measure up?

Now, halfway through the summer my son is relaxing in his new role. He is enjoying himself and his new earnings. At first I had to go with him to meet new customers. Now he insists on going alone. He has gained confidence enough to talk to people and deal with them by himself.

The money his job brings has purchased him a new radio and caused his small savings account to grow. He feels pride in the fact that he has satisfied his customers, and that some of them recommend him to their friends and family as a "good worker." He has taken the entire family out to dinner on his wages. This gives him a feeling of pride, of being "almost grown up."

Demands and threats, I found, are less effective than merely asking for a child's cooperation. When I emphasize my need for assistance, usually they are happy to lend a hand. Whenever one of them refuses to perform an assigned job, I try not to nag. There are better ways. If one of them is to feed the dog, for instance, and fails to perform this task, he or she is not allowed to play with the animal until it is taken care of. When dishes are not put away, that child reaps the natural consequences of his or her failure by not being allowed to sit down to eat until they are.

In the years from seven to twelve, a youngster comes to realize slowly that he is a responsible being. This dawning of truth is an ever-expanding trait. Wise parents support their children as they grow toward adult responsibility, bolstering them in their studies, household tasks, even play. Self-discipline and acceptance of responsibility are the marks of advancing maturity.

A child who refuses to accept tasks assigned, who scoffs at challenges, who refuses to do things for himself or others, becomes a deprived youngster. Such a child will never learn the satisfaction that comes from being self-reliant. As a youngster grows up he will eventually join the workaday world. It is then he will face many problems. Obstacles will be met and overcome. It is at this time teenagers need supportive parents to offer guidance, reassurance and love.

Work is a vital ingredient to a well-ordered life. A man at work is not a threat to anyone. A person committed to work becomes a constructive and creative member of society.

As John Wesley put it, "Do you labor to get your own living, abhorring idleness as you abhor hellfire? The devil tempts other men; but an idle man tempts the devil. An idle man's brain is the devil's shop, where he is continually working mischief."

In Closing . . .

Life is so daily, Lord. Help me to rise above the ordinariness of my tasks. Take me in hand, and guide me as I prepare this meal, discipline my child, communicate with my husband. I need Your guidance, Your presence, Your love. Help me to make my job a cooperative venture, with You, Lord, as director. Help me to see beyond the duties I tend to view as trivial, to take on Your perspective, to realize the eternal consequences of my occupation.